Super Soaps

Super Soaps
The Complete Book of Daytime Drama

**Jane Kutler and
Patricia Kearney**

Grosset & Dunlap
A Filmways Company
Publishers • New York

We wish to dedicate this book to several people, both individually and together.

First, to my parents, Blanche and Andrew Kutler, and my sister, Andra, whose priceless love, encouragement, and support have made me rich.

Second, to my parents, Constance and William Kearney, and my sisters, Connie and Jane, whom I love dearly.

And to Paul Denis, our "daytime father."

There are so many people to thank for their help in making this book happen that it is difficult to know where to begin.

First, to Jim Raftery of ABC, who so patiently put up with all our phone calls. To the producers of all the serials, especially Mary Bonner ("Another World"), Jeff Young and his assistant, Penny Eller ("The Doctors"), Thomas de Villiers ("Love of Life"), Claire Labine and Paul Avila Mayer ("Ryan's Hope"), Bud Kloss ("All My Children"), Doris Quinlan and Charlotte Weil ("One Life to Live") and Erwin Nicholson and Bud Gowen ("The Edge of Night").

To Betty Buchanan in Hollywood, who calmly took our calls of panic and provided us with the information we needed. Al Rosenberg, art director of *Daytime TV* and *Daylight TV,* will never know how much we appreciate his assistance in helping us put our ideas together.

And then there is Monty Sherman, for his beautiful photographs of the Hollywood stars.

And lastly, to the late Irna Phillips, for creating this marvelous art form in 1930.

Photographs on pp. 97-101 courtesy of "As the World Turns."

Copyright © 1977 by Jane Kutler and Patricia Kearney
All rights reserved
Published simultaneously in Canada
Library of Congress catalog card number: 76-48023
ISBN 0-448-12866-7 (hardcover edition)
ISBN 0-448-12860-8 (paperback edition)
First printing
Printed in the United States of America

Contents

Foreword vii

Part I Beginnings
   1. The Dawn of the Daytime Serial   3
   2. How Do They Write a Soap?   6

Part II The Serials
   3. Lovers and Friends   12
   4. Ryan's Hope   17
   5. Mary Hartman, Mary Hartman   23
   6. The Young and the Restless   31
   7. All My Children   41
   8. One Life to Live   51
   9. Days of Our Lives   60
  10. Another World   69
  11. The Doctors   76
  12. General Hospital   82
  13. The Edge of Night   89
  14. As the World Turns   95
  15. Guiding Light   102
  16. Love of Life   108
  17. Search for Tomorrow   115

Part III Beyond the Soap Suds
  18. A Day in the Life of a Soap   124
  19. They Are More Than Soap Stars   132
  20. The Famous Graduates   136
  21. The Emmy Awards   144

Appendix
   A Guide to All the Soaps That Ever Were   146

Index   149

Foreword

Unlike a play or a book, daytime drama is never really finished. The stories move from plot to plot, and the actors and characters shift constantly. Even if we had been able to place this book in your hands two weeks after writing it, many changes would have occurred. So we intend to give you in this book simply a background of the plots and the characters, hoping it will enhance your viewing pleasure.

Beyond the background material, many people are interested in knowing how a soap is conceived and written. As a matter of fact, so were we. For this reason we decided to interview Claire Labine and Paul Avila Mayer, the creators, head writers, and executive producers of "Ryan's Hope." Their show is so fresh that their experience is typical of today's network practices. They were most informative on the step-by-step process involved in this type of undertaking, and we are happy to pass along their comments.

One last word. Although many people, actors included, take exception to the word *soap,* we use it only with affection. It originated in the days when most of the dramatic serials were sponsored by soap companies. Today, daytime dramas are still given this label out of habit, but as the title of this book says, they are SUPER!

PART I
BEGINNINGS

1 The Dawn of the Daytime Serial

To the over fifty million people who watch daytime serials on television, it seems they have been around forever. In fact, the first serial was broadcast in 1946 and was planned for a limited run only. The most successful daytime TV drama in terms of longevity, "Search for Tomorrow," began broadcasting in 1951, and is still with us.

Television serials were a product of the last days of the "golden age of radio." At that time, the radio serial was generally looked upon as the housewife's companion, something she listened to while she did the ironing or cleaning. The serial was considered a low art form, just a way to give the woman at home pleasant distraction while she was doing her chores. Actors performed on daytime serials in order to earn money while waiting for their big break. That daytime serials would never succeed in television was the prevailing opinion; today, they are bigger and better than ever.

The serial form itself has been with us for a long time. The Greeks and Romans used it successfully in their myths. *Tales from the Arabian Nights* was surely a serial, and no less a novelist than Charles Dickens employed the serial format in his writings.

Roy Winsor, creator of "Search for Tomorrow" and "Love of Life," commented on this on the twenty-fifth anniversary of these shows in 1976:

"The serial is designed to build continuing interest and is actually an ancient literary form. The minstrels, and most likely Homer, told stories which ended each night on a note of expectancy, to be continued the next night."

Winsor continued, "Dickens wrote serials in the nineteenth-century fashion. His chapters are installments; all have related subplots and the reader is constantly left wondering what will happen next. A good story boils down to capturing a reader who cannot resist the temptation of the next chapter.

"Like a Dickens novel, a Greek epic, or 'The Arabian Nights,'" Winsor concluded, "a good serial stars with a basic premise. This is personified by one or more central characters. These characters encounter opposing attitudes and the result is conflict. And, conflict is drama."

The movies utilized the serial form for children. Flash Gordon, Hopalong Cassidy, Tom Mix, and Kit Carson would fill the theater screen every Saturday with the latest segment of interplanetary adventure or the fight to win the West.

But merely to serialize a story does not mean it will be a success. When "Painted Dreams," the first radio drama, by Irna Phillips, the queen of serial writing, was broadcast from Chicago in 1930, no one realized how successful the serial would become.

Television serials floundered until 1950, when "The First 100 Years" went out over the CBS network. Radio stars performed in the new format but rarely considered the medium worthy of their talent. "100 Years" lasted only one year.

At the end of that year, a few serials began that everyone could identify with. "Search for Tomorrow" started its run on September 3, 1951, and is still on the air. Some serials lasted only a short while, others were canceled after twenty years on the air.

Why do some shows develop a loyal following while others fail to attract any sizable audience? Basically, success is a matter of bringing to the viewing public a group of characters with whom ordinary people can identify. An important ingredient of any successful serial is a strong family unit with values and morals with which the viewing public can agree. Then, too, those in the audience must care about the people they watch. The characters cannot be walking zombies, without human emotions or feelings, without motivations for their behavior.

Each serial has its own way of capturing an audience. Often a new serial will open with a dramatic problem that the family must face together. Interestingly, if the problem is one that causes a negative response to the characters, the serial will usually fail. But, if the audience can relate to the problem, if it can identify with the way the characters react to their problem, then there is a good chance that the serial will succeed.

Other aspects must be considered by the network and writers of a new show. For example, what time will the show be on the air? If a serial is destined for the hours when teen-agers might be viewing, a youthful story line is accented. And some serials prefer to accentuate the personalities of the characters rather than the events that happen to them. Again, certain writers try to bring in "relevant" subject matter, hoping enlighten the views of their audience toward current issues.

Soaps fail when they lose believability. When the prohblems become too farfetched or a character's reaction to a problem is strictly "out of character," the audience loses its respect and love for a serial and finds another to take its place.

Very few radio shows were tried on television, and only one succeeded in making the transition. Perhaps this feat was accomplished because "Guiding Light" was broadcast both on radio and television for five years. This gave the listener a chance to become familiar with the faces behind the voices. Also, "Guiding Light" was broadcast first on radio and later that same day appeared on television. If you missed the radio show, you could tune in and watch what happened on the TV show. What better way to keep an audience happy?

Today's serials are enjoying a renaissance. Reviewers still pan them, but they are taking more notice of them. Their audience is widening, too. With more leisure time, men are often home during the day and are beginning to watch the shows. They are learning what women have known for years. The serials are more than tales to pass the time. They are carefully woven stories that keep the public informed about modern science and technology, that point out to people that help is available when someone suffers from one of the emotional problems so often depicted on the shows. The serials may also encourage a weak person to become stronger by living through his or her favorite character, by having a model from whom to learn how to face problems. And perhaps most important, they give the viewer isolated at home someone to care for. The characters do not remain mere actors saying lines and moving around a set. They become friends, revealing their innermost feelings and thoughts to millions of viewers.

The actors on the soaps also have warm feelings toward their fans. They know the importance of the job they do and respond with fine performances. Even when the audience doesn't like what certain characters are doing, if the actors get a rise out of the viewing public, they are doing it right.

It is about time that the serial earned the respect it has come to deserve. The serials have grown up, as has the country. Today's serials are intelligent, well-thought-out stories, enjoyable yet informative. They combine two important elements: people you can grow to love and care about; and that old cliff hanger, "What's going to happen next?"

2 How Do They Write a Soap?

According to the mountain of letters people send to the television networks, a sizable portion of the millions of people who watch daytime drama feel that they could write better serials than the professionals. Actually, writing a serial is a difficult task. And creating one is even more difficult. It takes many long hours and complete devotion, as Claire Labine and Paul Avila Mayer, the creators and head writers of "Ryan's Hope," can attest. Their account of how a show is developed and written may refer to "Ryan's Hope," but it is the universal story of any soap.

Claire Labine and Paul Mayer were writers of "Where the Heart Is" and "Love of Life" before they were approached by ABC about a new show. Both Paul and Claire are articulate, intelligent, and optimistic people, which is reflected in their show's characters. Interestingly, their Mary Ryan character is based on one of their writers, Mary Munisteri, whose maiden name was Ryan.

Paul begins the story of how "Ryan's Hope" was born:

"We were working for other people, and everyone has fantasies of wanting to work for themselves. We had things we wanted to try and would bitch to each other that we weren't allowed to write comedy or write story situations unless they were tried and true.

"In terms of this show, we were approached by ABC right after the writers' strike in 1973. First we sent ABC scripts and story breakdowns from "Where the Heart Is," and later they asked us if we would like to write a show called "City Hospital."

Both Paul and Claire have Irish heritages; the O'Neil family figures in both their ancestries. On "Where the Heart Is" they used an Irish bar as the setting for an affair between two of the show's characters and that story situation remained in the back of their minds until they were asked to develop a show of their own.

But the most important ingredient of any serial is people. Paul and Claire were to find out that developing characters and situations from scratch was even more difficult than they at first imagined. So, after thinking about ABC's request for a medical show, they returned to the network with their own proposal.

"We came back to ABC and said we wanted to write a show about a big Irish family who run a bar across the street from a city hospital. Claire and I like to write romantic stories. We are not too good on medical ones."

Then, according to Paul, "There were just an endless series of meetings. We talked out almost all of our ideas before we committed them to paper."

Once the story was developed in their own minds, writing what is known as the "bible" came next.

"We started with character," Paul explains. "We started with Johnny Ryan because he was the oldest person. We started with his father in about 1900. We figured out who his father was, and his mother, so that after Johnny Ryan was born in 1917, we traced his entire childhood through the twenties, thirties, the Second World War, his meeting Maeve, and so on. We brought all that into it."

"One of the things we find," Claire explains, "is that when we have one character who is defined, it is fun to define the other characters in opposition to that character, so you get complementary things going."

Claire Labine and Paul Avila Mayer are the creators, head writers, and executive producers of "Ryan's Hope."

How Do They Write a Soap? 7

Paul and Claire go over the long-term story, which is plotted out and interwoven month by month.

"When they said they would pay us for the bible," Paul recalls, "we thought that was nice. But when we finished the bible, we decided there wasn't enough money in the world to pay us for the work we had put into it. It was incredible. We worked every night, including Saturday and Sunday, for a year.

"It was hard because we would do a story, then do a new version of it, and then have a meeting with the network and do another version. After having written three versions of our own and three for the network, we had six versions of it in our heads and we would say, 'Which story did we decide on?'

"The bible was two hundred pages long. The first half was just back story, which was everything that had happened up to the point the show started. The second hundred pages were a story projection that covered about two years. After the first four weeks of the show, we threw it all out.

"We had wanted to open the show with the death of Frank Ryan and the impact on a big Irish family of the death of the favorite son. But the network said no one would understand why the people all cared so much. So, everything based on the death of Frank Ryan went out the window. If you have three stories projected, and they are all interlocking, and you change one entire story, it requires you to change all the others."

From the time ABC decided to go with "Ryan's Hope" on March 5, 1975, until the show premiered on July 7, 1975, all the casting, set building, and hiring of production staff had to be done.

Deciding on the title of a show is also a major decision. Paul reveals that he and Claire were successful in getting title approval for "Ryan's Hope" by waiting long enough. The network had tried to obtain the rights to "A Rage to Love," but when they were unable to clear the rights to use it, "Ryan's Hope" was settled on.

According to Paul, the title, "Ryan's Hope," is a generalization. "It is not just for any one of the Ryans or the Ryan family, but for all the people on the show. Claire has a wonderful way of expressing it: 'We wanted to write about people celebrating the human condition, rather than simply enduring it.'"

The day-to-day writing of a show is a taxing process. First, a long-term story projection must be drawn up. This document usually covers about one year of generalized story. After this is approved, the writers work out a more detailed outline, usually covering from six to eight weeks. Finally, each week is broken down, day by day, in an outline form from which the actual scripts are written.

"You can't get too far ahead because a lot of what we do is based on what we see on the screen," Paul explains. "Especially if we see two people working together and something is happening between them. Ideally the breakdowns should be five weeks ahead and the scripts three."

How are the story ideas developed, and do Claire and Paul ever worry about running out of ideas?

"I think you are always afraid," Paul says, "but we have never run dry in six years. Sometimes people will take a novel like *Jane Eyre* and just lift it. It's done a lot. But we get suggestions from Claire's mother, my wife, our children, everything we've ever read or seen—but what we're looking for are big stories with steps."

"We don't panic," Claire interjects. "Actually there are two ways to do it. The sudden inspiration in the bathtub—the bolt out of the blue is wonderful when it happens. And it has happened to us, maybe, three times.

"Then there is the situation," she continues, "where you sit down and say, 'You have Mary and Jack in this situation and Seneca, Frank, and Jill in their situation, and given these people, what would happen next?' Then you say, 'All right, this would happen, but it's not very interesting. How do you complicate it?' The story really just sort of emerges. You build it. But, as to how it is done, I really don't know. By the grace of God," she concludes.

As a successful writing team, each one has a favorite type of scene they like to write. "Paul really wants a story that moves," Claire explains. "He wants conflict in scenes and a story that's moving. And I want endless scenes between Mary and her mother." And each hopes that that favorite scene is the reason the show is a success.

"The combination is simply wonderful because neither of us is completely right," Paul says. "The ongoing interest is maintained by what's going to happen next. Both things work together."

Once a show is on the air and successful, that is not the end of it. The complaint from viewers that stories occasionally don't move quickly enough must often be dealt with. Paul and Claire are aware of this aspect, but from a writer's point of view, it is a problem to be waited out.

"You want to tell a good story," Paul points out, "and sometimes, if you think of the show as a long-running novel, then you think of stories with lots of steps in them. If you have stories with many steps, then you're golden. If you have stories with maybe four big emotional progresses, they're very hard to write. Inevitably, you get into repeating the same kind of situation. Even if you put a lot of time and effort into trying to develop incidents and be ingenious, you don't hide from the audience the fact that it's moving slowly and not much is happening.

"Sometimes you look at something and you see the next step is two months away. Nothing is going to change for eight weeks. You can't take your next step because it is interlocked with one of your other stories. It's hard just trying to keep it alive."

Having been through the development of this show, Paul

Every detail of the show is gone over by Paul, Claire, and the show's producer, Robert Costello.

and Claire are unanimous in feeling that they do not want to develop another one.

"Claire once said that it was inconceivable to her that there was a more difficult job anywhere in the world, in terms of emotional effort involved in the hours and lack of sleep and relentless pressure," Paul comments.

"And you're afraid to stop caring," Claire responds. "The second you start to get cynical, something happens that really pulls you up short.

"There are so many things that mitigate against quality in a daytime show, time being the primary one. When you really start analyzing the problems, you realize it's impossible to do it well. You cannot do a quality daytime show—and yet it is done. And the only way it is done is by somebody breaking his neck. That's really what it amounts to. And everybody around here does break his neck."

Do you still think you can tackle the problems of writing a soap better than the show's creators and writers?

10   BEGINNINGS

PART II
THE SERIALS

3 Lovers and Friends

On January 3, 1977, the youngest member of the fourteen-strong world of daytime dramas, "Lovers and Friends," premiered. No details about the opening plot were revealed until the program hit the airways, although the show was on the drawing board for a full year before making its debut.

Harding (Pete) Lemay and Paul Rauch developed this show for Procter & Gamble and the NBC television network. Rauch and Lemay are not newcomers to the daytime scene. As executive producer and head writer, respectively, for another NBC drama, "Another World," they pioneered the hour-long daytime serial and have consistently maintained high placement in the temperamental Nielsen ratings.

Using "Another World" as a blueprint for success, "Lovers and Friends" showcased top-notch acting against a background of lavish sets. Psychological development of character, rather than social issues or fast-moving plots, was stressed.

This new serial took over the NBC Brooklyn studio that formerly housed the ill-fated "Somerset." Not so coincidentally, this enormous network complex is also home for "Another World"; Rauch and Lemay will be able to keep close contact with their two creations.

"Lovers and Friends" is set in a fashionable Chicago suburb, Point Claire, an area resembling the real town of Lake Forest, Illinois. The story line revolves around the interrelationships of three generations of two neighboring families: the affluent Cushings and the struggling Saxtons.

Heading the Cushing clan is patriarch Richard, a successful stockbroker, to all appearances a stolid, respectable businessman. But financial success has afforded Richard what he considers a luxurious necessity: Barbara Manners, who doubles as his executive secretary and mistress. Richard's wife, Edith, relishes the Cushing status and wealth and frowns on anyone outside her social circle.

Despite Edith and Richard's wealth, they have been unable to discover the secret of raising their two children into mature, self-sufficient adults. Austin, their twenty-five-year-old son, is an unemployed college dropout who drinks too much and looks for work too little. But his major source of distress is an overbearing mother who interferes in his life. Megan, their twenty-two-year-old daughter, is a recent college graduate currently taking journalism courses. But she, too, has been spoiled by her family.

Adding a touch of down-to-earth humor to the Cushing household is Edith's mother, Sophia Slocum. She's a woman uninhibited by wealth or upper-class pretensions, who tries her best to add a touch of reality to her children's lives.

Megan's parents are delighted with her engagement to wealthy Desmond Hamilton, but the bride-to-be is a bit reluctant. Love is not a main ingredient in this relationship, and Megan is trying to convince herself that their social status is well matched, thus making their future marriage a success.

Austin Cushing appeared to lose his most prized possession when his love affair with Laurie Brewster came to an end. Laurie, who is Megan's best friend, could not tolerate Austin's pose of social superiority and lethargic attitude toward the work ethic; she needed a man who was more ambitious. Laurie's grandmother took her to Europe to try and forget the past.

Living next door to the Cushings are the less affluent Saxtons. Husband and father Lester is a reformed alcoholic who has had to work hard for every penny he has ever possessed. Out of work for six months, he finally secured a job as a warehouse manager and was able to afford the move to this wealthy neighborhood.

Lester's wife, Josie, is an affable woman who believes in the importance of family and faith. She was delighted to move to her luxurious new home, a delight not always shared by her children.

The Saxtons are the parents of five offspring. The eldest, twenty-seven-year-old Eleanor, is married to a kind and understanding man named George Kimball. Always ashamed of her poor upbringing, Eleanor has struggled to get her parents to change their lower-class standards. The remaining Saxton brood are: Rhett, twenty-four, a free-spirit photographer engaged to Connie Ferguson; Jason, twenty-two; Bentley, eighteen; and Tessa, fifteen. Eleanor and Rhett are happy to see their parents moving into a higher social class, but Tessa and Bentley feel out of place in their new surroundings and yearn to return to their former life style.

Also living with the Saxtons is cousin Amy Gifford. Amy is a kind, family-conscious young woman with firm convictions and

The alcoholic Austin Cushing is played by Rod Arrants.

Lovers and Friends 13

The stuffy matriarch of the Cushing family, Edith, is portrayed by Nancy Marchand.

Margaret Barker is a veteran actress and adds a touch of humor as the rich Sophia Slocum.

high ideals. But she's having second thoughts about whether she cares to continue with her current living arrangement.

Richard Cushing is portrayed by actor Ron Randell. His impressive acting credentials include hosting two of London's leading TV shows, "On the Town" and "What's My Line?" He was seen on Broadway in starring roles in *The World of Suzie Wong, The Browning Version,* and *Candide.* He has appeared in several nighttime television series, among them "Bewitched" and "The Outer Limits."

Talented actress Nancy Marchand portrays Edith Cushing. A respected stage actress, she has received the critics' praise for starring roles in the Broadway productions *Forty Carats* and *After the Rain.* Nancy and her husband, actor Paul Sparer, live in Manhattan.

While her role as Megan Cushing marks Patricia Estrin's first continuing role on a daytime drama, this young actress is by no means a newcomer to television. In Hollywood she guested on numerous nighttime series, such as "The Mary Tyler Moore Show," "Doc," "Police Woman," and "Barnaby Jones." She has starred in regional theater productions of *Who's Afraid of Virginia Woolf?, The Lark, You Can't Take It with You, Romeo and Juliet,* and many more.

If actress Dianne Harper looks familiar from roles other than her Laurie Brewster part, perhaps you've seen her on "Happy Days," "The Rockford Files," or "Serpico."

The character of Sophia Slocum is brilliantly portrayed by actress Margaret Barker. A veteran of the Broadway stage, she has been delighting theatergoers for forty-eight years, having made her professional debut in 1928 in *The Age of Innocence,* which starred Katharine Cornell. In fact, Miss Barker's stage credits are endless. And she has previously appeared on the daytime serials "Love of Life," "Edge of Night," and "The Doctors."

Lester Saxton is portrayed by John Heffernan. An outstanding stage actor, he made his Broadway debut succeeding Albert Finney in the title role in *Luther.* Heffernan won the Variety Critics' Award for his supporting role in *Tiny Alice* and drew raves for work in *Bad Habits, Purlie,* and *Postmark Zero.* His impressive film credits include roles in *The Sting* and *The Time of the Heathen.* On television, you may have seen him in episodes of "All in the Family," "Maude," or as the mad bomber in "Mary Hartman, Mary Hartman."

Although her part as Josie Saxton marks Patricia Englund's daytime debut, she has appeared on television in several capacities: as an actress in the early 1960s on "That Was the Week

14   THE SERIALS

Noted stage actor John Heffernan is Lester Saxton. He was also the "mad bomber of Fernwood" on "Mary Hartman, Mary Hartman."

Patricia Englund, who plays Josie Saxton, a warm, loving mother.

Rhett Saxton is portrayed by handsome David Ramsey.

That Was," and as an NBC-TV weather girl! Happily married with a family, Patricia is the sister-in-law of actress Cloris ("Phyllis") Leachman. She starred in the original Broadway productions of *Oklahoma!* and *As You Like It.*

Eleanor Saxton Kimball is played by Flora Plumb, who has appeared in countless nighttime TV series, including "Police Story," "Mannix," "Mod Squad," and "Marcus Welby, M.D." Her film credits include *On a Clear Day You Can See Forever* and *Run, Shadow Run.*

Portraying George Kimball is veteran star of stage and screen Stephen Joyce. Recognizable from previous daytime serial roles on "Love Is a Many Splendored Thing," "As the World Turns," and "Search for Tomorrow," he is also an accomplished stage actor and won the Theater World Award for his performance in *Stephen D.*

Handsome Rhett Saxton is portrayed by David Ramsey, a University of Iowa graduate whose varied interests range from karate to horseback riding to gymnastics. Previously, Ramsey appeared on "Love of Life," in the film *Crazy Joe,* and in the Broadway production of *Equus.* This six-foot bachelor resides in Manhattan.

Lovers and Friends 15

Newcomer Richard Backus portrays Jason Saxton.

A normal teen-ager in real life, Vicky Dawson plays Tessa Saxton, who is also a normal teen-ager.

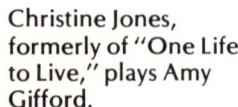

Christine Jones, formerly of "One Life to Live," plays Amy Gifford.

Immediately before Richard Backus won the role of Jason Saxton, he scored on TV in a starring role in "Ah, Wilderness!" He was also seen in the NBC-TV special "Judge Horton and the Scottsboro Boys." On Broadway, he appeared in *Butterflies Are Free* and won the Theater World Award for his role in *Promenade All*.

The youngest Saxton, Tessa, is portrayed by Vicky Dawson. You may have seen her on any one of the many television specials in which she has appeared: "It Must Be Love Because I Feel So Dumb," "Rookie of the Year," and the TV movie "After He's Gone." Vicky also played the title role in "Sybil Luddington" on the NBC series "GO-USA."

Actress Christine Jones, recently divorced, is familiar to daytime audiences from past roles on "One Life to Live" and "Love of Life." Her theater credits include regional and college productions; on Broadway she appeared in *All the Girls Came Out to Play*.

16   THE SERIALS

4
Ryan's Hope

"Ryan's Hope" is ABC's newest serial, having made its debut July 7, 1975. Unlike most other daytime dramas, "Ryan's Hope" stresses reality in character, situation, and location. The show's setting is Riverdale, New York, an area of New York City that is almost suburban in tone.

As its title suggests, the story line concentrates on two Irish immigrants—Johnny and Maeve Ryan—who met and fell in love in Ireland while he was serving with the European Theater of Operations in World War II. Armed with little more than their dreams and hopes for the future, they came to America and settled in Riverdale.

Tony Award winner Helen Gallagher and daytime veteran Bernard Barrow are Maeve and Johnny Ryan.

A proud, basically self-educated man, Johnny has always believed in earning his way and taking handouts from no one. He has worked his way up from jobs as a bouncer in a bar to bar manager and now owns his own bar, which bears the family name.

Maeve is warm, loving, and a bit more tolerant than her husband. Because she is a sentimentalist and he a disciplinarian, life for their five children—Frank, Patrick, Mary, Siobhan, and Kathleen—is interesting, to say the least!

The eldest Ryan son, Frank, had intended to put the Ryan name on the American map. Highly educated, his charisma and concern for people made him an idealistic young political candidate. Only one obstacle blocked a potentially bright future: his neurotic wife, Delia.

Frank and Delia have known each other since childhood and were married relatively young. At first Frank was attracted to Delia's helplessness and dependency, as his innate need to help others transcended his personal life. Frank felt Delia could not survive without him.

For the first time in her life, Delia felt she had an identity. As a Ryan, she was somebody. Frank and Delia have a son, Johnny, but even the joys of fatherhood faded as Frank grew intolerant of his wife's constant whining and lack of independence.

Frank became romantically involved with beautiful young lawyer Jill Coleridge, the antithesis of Delia. He was drawn to Jill's sensitivity as well as her highly independent nature. They were

The culprits of the show: Ron Hale and Ilene Kristin as Dr. Roger Coleridge and Delia Ryan.

18 THE SERIALS

lovers and desperately wanted to marry. But Frank's marriage and his devout religious upbringing had to be considered. Realizing, too, that the affair would prove a definite political liability, they decided to wait until after Frank's City Council election was over before proceeding with any personal plans.

Delia, who knew of the affair, became close to Jill's half-brother, Dr. Roger Coleridge. A vindictive man, Roger was capable of infinite cruelty. He would stoop to any depths in order to get what he wanted. And yet, while Roger nurtured Delia's deep-seated emotional problems, he truly loved her.

Wanting Delia for himself, Roger set out to destroy Frank's political future so that Frank would no longer delay his divorce. Roger informed a news reporter of Frank's extramarital affair, which brought Frank under public scrutiny.

Jill had represented Frank in his custody fight for little John, but another pressing matter was on her mind. She had defended Dr. Seneca Beaulac against a charge of manslaughter after he switched off his fatally ill wife's life-supporting device in the hospital. (Roger Coleridge had turned Seneca in to the authorities.) Following Seneca's conditional acquittal, he and Jill had spent a weekend at her beachhouse seeking solitude and rest. They made love one night, and she became pregnant with his child. Morally, Jill could not abort the baby. And she felt Seneca had a right to know of his child's existence, although she realized Frank was the only man she had ever loved.

If Andrew Robinson had not become an actor, he says he might have been a politician, like his character, Frank Ryan.

Maeve and Johnny Ryan thought Delia would end up marrying a Ryan all right—but they did not think it would be Frank. Throughout their childhood, Delia and Frank's brother, Patrick, were very close. To this day, a strong emotional bond binds the two; frequently, Pat is the only one who understands and tolerates Delia's erratic behavior.

Because Pat related to people so well, he chose a medical career. He was outgoing and attractive and many girls tried to win his affections, but Pat enjoyed playing the field.

One young woman who was drawn to him was his fellow physician, Dr. Faith Coleridge, sister of Dr. Roger Coleridge and half-sister to Jill. Before meeting Pat, she had been afraid of romantic involvement. The only man in her life was her father, but after he died she was free to pursue her own happiness. Faith fell for Pat's cocky self-assurance and independence. They became lovers, but when he realized she wanted exclusive rights to him, Pat cooled their relationship to a friendship.

Once Faith stopped actively chasing him, Pat realized how important she was to him. They resumed casual dating. Meanwhile, Delia realized that a future with Frank was impossible and, determined to remain a Ryan, she set her sights on Pat.

The third Ryan offspring, Mary, has not had much better

Ryan's Hope

luck with her personal life than her two older brothers have had. While working on brother Frank's campaign, she met and fell in love with newspaper reporter Jack Fenelli.

Mary had never known anyone quite like Jack, and no wonder! They were from opposite walks of life. While Mary had been raised in a warm, loving family atmosphere, Jack had grown up in an orphanage. The only person he learned to trust and depend on was himself.

Through patience and compassion, Mary taught him all about loyalty to loved ones. This kind of all-encompassing love was something totally new for Jack Fenelli. He resented the feeling of needing someone.

When Mary began work at a local television station and her boss took a liking to her, Jack became torn with jealousy. He reluctantly proposed—she readily accepted. Mary's parents had bitterly disapproved when she and Jack began living together, but they had remained relatively silent in order not to lose a daughter.

A close-knit family, the Ryans go to one another with their problems; here, Kate Mulgrew and Malcolm Groome as Mary Ryan Fenelli and Pat Ryan.

The marriage almost never got off the ground. Jack had last-minute doubts and came close to stranding Mary at the altar. He sheepishly arrived two hours late.

Their marriage has been an on-again, off-again love affair. Jack demands Mary reduce her dependence on her family. Mary desperately wants children, but Jack says they have no place in his life. (Her unanticipated pregnancy made him feel betrayed.)

20 THE SERIALS

While "Ryan's Hope" represents Helen Gallagher's serial debut, it didn't take this talented actress long to make her mark in daytime TV. Honored in 1975 with an Emmy Award as daytime TV's best actress for her role as Maeve Ryan, she has also received a Tony Award for her role on Broadway in *No, No, Nanette*. Currently separated from her TV executive husband, Helen lives on Manhattan's Upper West Side, where she conducts weekly classes in acting and musical comedy. A delightfully warm, unpretentious lady, she says that acting and the theater are both her career and hobby, and that children are her favorite people.

Helen and Bernard Barrow, who plays Johnny Ryan, are close friends. Their cameraderie is apparent on the air. Perhaps Bernie is such a fine actor because he is familiar with so many different aspects of his profession. For the past twenty-seven years he has taught Drama and Theater Arts; in 1976 he was awarded his full professorship at Brooklyn College. He possesses a warm sense of humor and is ecstatically happy with his wife, actress Joan Kaye. They divide their time between two residences: an East Side Manhattan apartment and a spacious country home situated in eastern Pennsylvania. Bernie remains close to his two children from a first marriage, Susan and Tom.

Of his role as Frank Ryan, actor Andrew Robinson says, "If there's any prototype for him [Frank], it's John F. Kennedy." Ironically, at one time, Andrew considered entering politics: "Up until I graduated from school, I wanted to be Secretary of State!" He has appeared in over fifty plays, guested on countless nighttime TV series, and made his film debut in *Dirty Harry*, which starred Clint Eastwood. Andrew and his wife of seven years, Irene, live in Manhattan with their four-year-old daughter, Rachel, and one of Irene's two sons from a previous marriage, seventeen-year-old Daniel. Andrew is a firm advocate of astrology. To relax, he enjoys tap dancing and tennis.

Patrick Ryan calls Riverdale, New York, home. But for the actor who created him, Malcolm Groome, that's not such an easy task. As the son of a military man, Malcolm and his family lived in several areas of the world. Right now, he's happily settled in New York, where he pursues his stage and film career. Single, he does not rule out the possibility of marriage.

Ilene Kristin's free-flowing blonde hair and brilliant blue eyes give her a striking appearance. Her convincing portrayal of the neurotic Delia Ryan reveals her as a truly talented actress. Although "Ryan's Hope" was her first major continuing television role, an acting career was no fly-by-night decision—she's wanted it since the tender age of four! Unlike her role, she's a genuinely independent spirit. For the past several years, she's been romantically involved with actor-singer Joey Ward. They both reside in Manhattan apartments but frequently escape to an upstate New York farm,

As Pat Ryan, Malcolm Groome is a man caught in the middle.

Ryan's Hope 21

where they go to auctions, hunt for antiques, and just enjoy the serenity.

The person with probably the most expressive eyes on the daytime scene is Nancy Addison, who plays Jill Coleridge.

Ilene Kristin and John Gabriel (Dr. Seneca Beaulac) watch their fellow actors' performances.

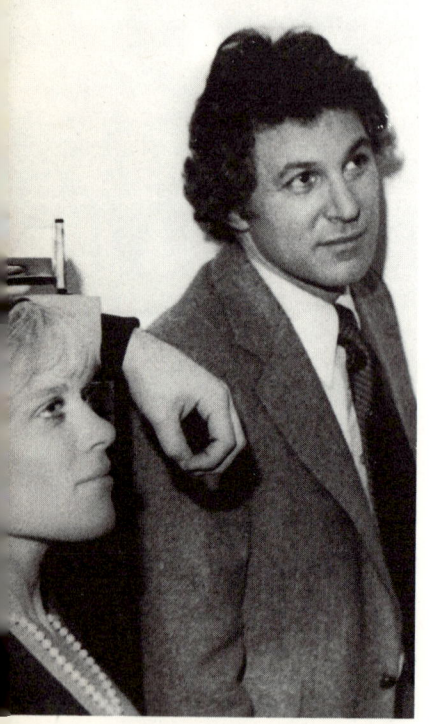

Beautiful Nancy Addison, who portrays Jill Coleridge, has an insatiable thirst for knowledge; she likes reading, karate, guitar, visiting flea markets, attending plays. Single and living in Manhattan, Nancy is currently dating businessman Howard Linker, with whom she attended high school.

Dr. Seneca Beaulac may be unable to win his lady love on "Ryan's Hope," but in real life, the actor who portrays him, John Gabriel, has no such problem. He and his attractive wife, Sandy, reside in midtown Manhattan with their two daughters, seven-year-old Melissa and four-year-old Ondi. John has proven himself successful in many phases of his business: stage, nighttime television, and recording.

Twenty-two and ready to conquer the world—that's Kate Mulgrew! She enjoys her role as Mary Ryan Fenelli but also is intent on establishing a successful stage career. While she's single at the moment, she hopes one day to marry and have a large family. She resides on Manhattan's Upper West Side and is seriously dating aspiring film director Ben Levitt, whom Kate describes as "the most wonderful person I've ever met."

Ruggedly handsome Michael Levin knew he wanted a career in the arts but seriously considered writing before deciding on the acting field. Outgoing, with a wonderful sense of humor, this actor, who plays Jack Fenelli, lives with his wife, Elizabeth, and their three sons—Aaron, Jason, and Scott. Michael stays in shape by skiing, jogging, and playing basketball.

22 THE SERIALS

5
Mary Hartman, Mary Hartman

Norman Lear decided to produce a soap opera, but it took over seven years for his idea to materialize. Lear wanted actors who could be both funny and serious at the same time. And he wanted to tell true stories and yet be able to poke fun.

To poke fun at an institution can be a high form of flattery. Everyone should be able to laugh at himself every now and again. And the new form to laugh at was that "American institution," the soap opera.

Lear knew what kind of heroine he wanted after he saw the film *Slither,* starring Louise Lasser. But it wasn't until the character of Mary was developed that Lasser was called in to audition. She turned Lear down—at first. She didn't understand what he was trying to do. Then she reconsidered and decided to put her television fate in the hands of the king of situation comedy.

ABC was interested in Lear's new project and gave him a small amount of money to help with it. Then they backed down. CBS was the next network to give support to Lear; they funded the pilot of "Mary Hartman, Mary Hartman." Then CBS, too, turned away. Never one to say die, Lear and his associates set about selling "Mary" to the various independent networks. On a landmark day in television history—January 5, 1975—"Mary Hartman" made her debut. And she was a resounding success.

Although "Mary" is not a soap in the traditional sense of the word, there is no other way to describe it. "Mary" is a soap in the sense that problems are never ending and highly entertaining.

Mary and Tom Hartman cannot be called stupid people. Their only fault is that they live in a small town and their personal horizons are limited. But small-town people have problems, too.

The major industry of Fernwood, Ohio, is the automobile assembly plant. But our hapless hero, Tom, manages to lose his job because of a drinking problem. He also has an affair. Mary finds

Louise Lasser, who plays our heroine, Mary Hartman.
© Copyright T.A.T. Communications Company. All rights reserved.

Breakfast at the Hartmans with Heather (Claudia Lamb), Mary (Lasser), and Tom (Mullavey).
© Copyright T.A.T. Communications Company. All rights reserved.

both problems too large to handle, and she has a nervous breakdown, right on David Susskind's show.

With Mary away, Tom begins to straighten out his life. For the first time in all his working years, he starts wearing a suit; he rises to success as a salesman of family recreational vehicles. Mary's breakdown is short-lived and while in the sanitarium, she meets some new friends.

Tom's horizons have been expanding since his success in business. He is more aware of the world outside Fernwood, and his life has taken on wider horizons than his once-a-week bowling league.

Mary is trying to understand her family. She has secretly admitted she is afraid of her daughter, Heather, and is thrilled to consider herself a close friend of writer Gore Vidal. Mary is a devoted friend and model housewife and mother.

A true heroine, Mary even saved the state of Ohio from being blown up. But her basic insecurities about her husband, since his affair, keep coming to the surface whenever Tom talks about his friend Annie Wylie, better known to CBers as Tippy-Toes.

Mary's long-suffering mother, Martha Shumway, was anxious to find out about her real father. Billy Twelvetrees, who responded to her ad, was uncovered as the most likely candidate. Although Martha was happy to have found him, the discovery did not detract from her relationship with her adopted father, Grandpa Larkin, once known as the "Fernwood Flasher."

24   THE SERIALS

Martha lived happily in her world of family and friends, never one to worry too much about problems, probably because she had trouble understanding them. Her blind faith kept her going.

But suddenly Martha had to take charge. Her husband and provider, George, disappeared while walking around the back of the car to open Martha's door for her. On top of that, her youngest daughter, Kathy, discovered she was pregnant, with no available father in sight.

Martha, gullible as ever, hoped that Jack and Jane, two con artists appearing briefly in the series, were right when they said George had been kidnapped by a space ship. But Detective Johnson managed to get Jack and Jane away from Martha. It appeared Detective Johnson might not want George to be found anyway.

Martha decided to become an actress in police-training films to help supplement the family's dwindling bank account. And Kathy arranged to sell her baby. She was also offered more money if, after the birth of her first child, she would agree to become impregnated by Brian Addams. And Grandpa found a job to help out also.

The May—December marriage of Loretta and Charlie Haggers hit some snags recently. Loretta, all of twenty-two, dreamed of being a Country-Western superstar, and Charlie had complete confidence that she would be.

Because of a layoff at the plant, Charlie lost his job. But

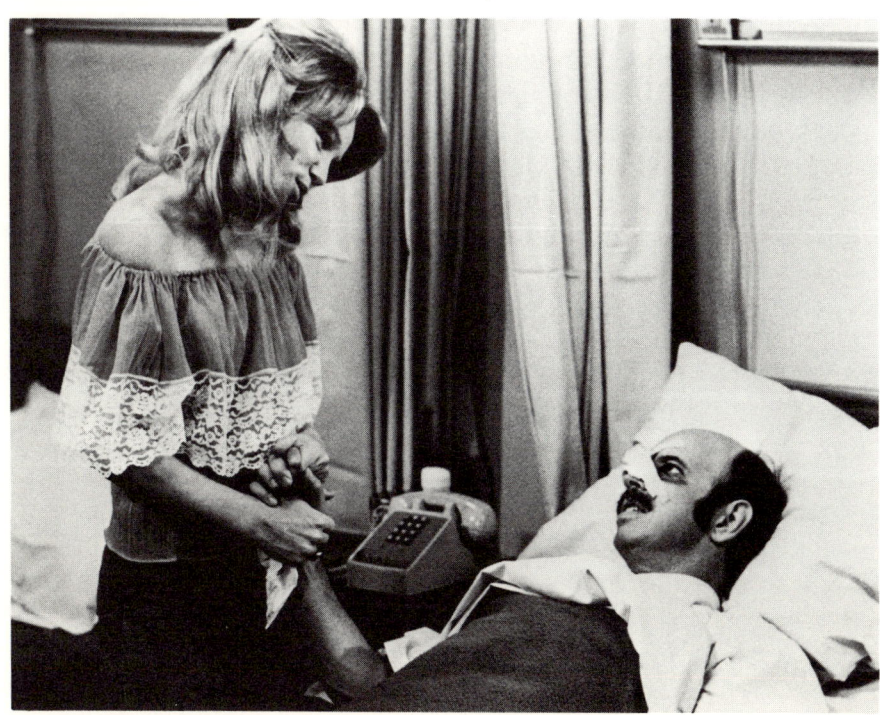

Now that Charlie (Graham Jarvis) has recovered from his accident, Loretta (Mary Kay Place) is missing.

© Copyright T.A.T. Communications Company. All rights reserved.

Mary Hartman, Mary Hartman

that was only the beginning of his troubles. Charlie was suspicious that Merle Jeeter was after Loretta's "young and firm" body. When Charlie went to the motel where Loretta was being seduced by Merle, an accident followed. Charlie was shot, losing part of his manhood and breaking his nose.

Sure that the good life with Loretta was over, even though Loretta kept trying to tell him his impairment was only temporary, Charlie answered an ad in the back of a "questionable" magazine, for a transplant.

It was with high hopes that Charlie left to have his operation, but Loretta wasn't as optimistic. He didn't know that his transplant donor was not a Dane—it was a Great Dane, to be exact. And Charlie ended up more than just a victim of fraud; he ended up in jail on charges of cruelty to animals. The doctor of his hopes was a vet. Destroyed were his plans of getting more than just his hopes up. In despair, Charlie called Loretta and told her he was never coming back. She should forget him and start her life over again.

Looking for friendship in a new town is all that Annie Wylie can be accused of. But Mary doesn't see it that way when it comes to her husband. Annie's desires are not centered on Tom; she has her sights set on a very sexy man, Merle Jeeter.

Merle has been trying to repent since his wandering days. He is sorry for what happened to Charlie, and since the death of his son, the Reverend Jimmy Joe Jeeter, by electrocution when the television set fell into the bathtub while Jimmie Joe was bathing, Merle has decided to follow through on his dreams to build his Condos for Christ.

But Wanda Rittenhouse has other ideas for Merle's future. She sees him as a possible political candidate and lover. Trying to capture Merle in bed has not been one of Wanda's major success stories. Merle has told her that she turns him off.

Merle did succumb to Annie, and while Annie found the whole episode very normal and healthy, Merle is afraid he is becoming a philanderer again. This is the only fault in his character he has promised himself to overcome.

Mary's nurse at the sanitarium was Pat Gimble. Pat was a curiosity because she always managed to report to work with some sort of new bruise or broken bone. But Pat always had a clear, though illogical, excuse for her mishaps.

Upon her release, Mary was pleased when Pat and her husband, Garth, bought a house on her block. Everything seemed fine at the Gimble home, until Garth was revealed in his true colors. He was an overdemanding man, subject to abusing his wife when he felt he was not getting his way.

Pat quietly took his abuse, but began to get fed up. Garth's cruelty may have temporarily been diverted into new direc-

His Condos for Christ gambit has been shelved as Merle (Dabney Coleman) embarks on a political career.
© Copyright T.A.T. Communications Company. All rights reserved.

26   THE SERIALS

Mary and Tom Hartman (Louise Lasser and Greg Mullavey) often talk over their problems in bed.
© Copyright T.A.T. Communications Company. All rights reserved.

tions. He forced Pat to quit her job and stay home, since he promised not to hit her again. But Pat's troubles began to multiply when Garth was accidentally killed with the top of their Christmas tree and Pat was arrested for his murder.

The former wife of Woody Allen, Louise Lasser never had to live the type of life Mary does. Born and raised in New York, she is the daughter of a tax consultant and always went to private schools. When the acting bug hit, Louise studied with the best instructors possible, Sanford Meisner and Elaine May. The fast pace and one-show-a-day production are exhausting, but Louise is taking it in stride and is pulling hard for Mary.

If you ask him, Greg Mullavey can relate to his character of Tom. Greg grew up in a small town like Tom's, and at one time he worked on an assembly line. Greg turned to acting on a dare; his first professional job was in the off-Broadway production of *Ah, Wilderness*. From there on it was hard work to perfect his craft and find other jobs in the not-so-stable acting world. Greg and his wife, actress Meredith MacRae, are the proud parents of a three-year-old daughter and have also started their own production company. Their first endeavor is a film called *My Friends Need Killing*.

Dody Goodman (Martha Shumway) first came into national prominence on Jack Paar's show. But Dody did not start out as an actress. She was a dancer first. It was during the road tour of *Wonderful Town* that Imogene Coca encouraged Dody to give up dancing and develop her flair for comedy. Not only a great comedienne, Dody has written several scripts, among them "Mourning in a Funny Hat" and "Women, Women, Women."

Mary Hartman, Mary Hartman

When Debralee Scott was in high school in her hometown of Tenafly, New Jersey, one of her teachers told her she would never become a star. It would be interesting to find out what this teacher's comments are now, since Debralee can be seen every night as Kathy Shumway. As Debralee's talents became more in demand, she moved to Hollywood, where the action was. After several TV movies playing poignant teen-agers, such as "Lisa Bright and Dark" and "Summer Without Boys," she had a recurring role on "Welcome Back, Kotter," playing Hotsie-Totsie.

Believe it or not, Grandpa Larkin is eighty-six years old. But Victor Kilian, who plays Grandpa, is eighty-six years young. Born in New Jersey, Kilian began his career at the age of eighteen. His Broadway debut was in the original production of Eugene O'Neill's *Desire Under the Elms*. Then movies called him, but his permanent move to Hollywood did not happen until 1970, when he joined his sister and son there. Kilian says he has always played character parts, usually "heavies." "Even when I was very young," he says, "I used to portray old men. And believe me—I'm amused when I remember how I thought how they should be."

George Shumway may have disappeared for a while, but actor Philip Bruns was keeping busy. He has business interests in both the United States and Europe. Bruns is no newcomer to the daytime audience; he has appeared on "The Secret Storm," "Love

Mary's family and friends. *Back row:* Greg Mullavey, Dody Goodman, Louise Lasser, Victor Kilian. *Front row:* Claudia Lamb, Philip Bruns and Debralee Scott.
© Copyright T.A.T. Communications Company. All rights reserved.

28 THE SERIALS

of Life," and "As the World Turns." His movie credits include *The Great Waldo Pepper, Harry and Tonto, Midnight Cowboy,* and *A Thousand Clowns.* Once an athlete, Bruns was born in Pipestone, Minnesota, and has been seen in twenty-six off-Broadway plays, six Broadway plays, and nearly six hundred commercials.

Keeping busy is Mary Kay Place's motto. Her role of Loretta Haggers has provided Mary Kay with an excellent opportunity to display her musical talents. She writes most of the songs she sings as Loretta. She recorded her first album, as Loretta, and has plans for a second, as herself. Her songwriting talents are only one aspect of her writing talents. Mary Kay has co-scripted episodes of "Phyllis," "Rhoda," "Maude," and "The Mary Tyler Moore Show." She and her co-writer were nominated for an Emmy for a script that they did for "M*A*S*H."

The bruises on Graham Jarvis' face at the beginning of last season were his own. No makeup department could have done such an authentic job on Charlie Haggers. Graham had been in an automobile accident prior to his second season, and the writers ingeniously incorporated his injuries into the story. Luckily, neither Graham, his wife, nor their infant son were seriously injured in the accident. Graham's career has spanned Broadway, films, and nighttime programs. But before success came his way, he had to work as a change-maker at a 42nd Street penny arcade and as a door-to-door salesman of encyclopedias.

To soap opera fans, Dabney Coleman is not a new face. He is remembered for his role as Dr. Tracy Graham on "Bright Promise." Since the cancellation of that soap, Dabney's career has centered around nighttime shows and movies. But never before has he played such a religious, lustful man as Merle Jeeter. Coleman plays his part to perfection. He's is married to actress Jean Hale and they are the parents of two children, Randolph and Kelly. Before becoming an actor, Coleman studied law. One of his more recent films was *The Other Side of the Mountain.* He is a descendant of Declaration of Independence signer John Randolph.

Star of stage, movies, and television Gloria DeHaven was on a soap once before: "As the World Turns." She is an individualist, just like her character of Annie Wylie. Gloria comes from a distinguished theatrical family; her parents were known as Mr. and Mrs. Carter DeHaven on stage and in the movies. Gloria made her own film debut as a child, appearing in Charlie Chaplin's *Modern Times.* Her sultry voice made her a natural for the bands, and she sang with Bob Crosby's orchestra before she was once again discovered by the movies. She was one of Frank Sinatra's first leading ladies in films.

Although Pat may have been afraid of her husband Garth, there is no need to fear Martin Mull, who played him. A fine stand-up comic, this was Mull's first acting role. He was discovered by

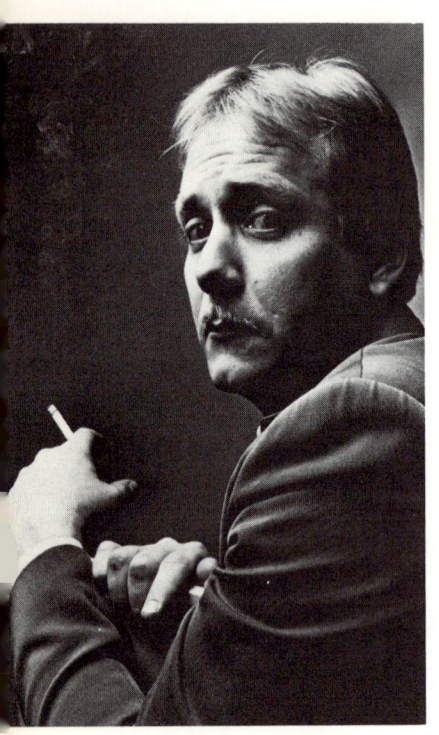

Wife-beater Garth is actually stand-up comic Martin Mull.
© Copyright T.A.T. Communications Company. All rights reserved.

Norman Lear and Al Burton while performing at The Roxy, one of Hollywood's leading rock hangouts. Martin is once again entering the bachelor world. Originally from Ohio, most of his life he has lived and worked in New York. He has recorded four hit comedy albums; his latest, "I'm Everyone I Ever Loved" (ABC Records), has just been released.

Who would not feel sympathy and compassion for Pat Gimble, once you looked into those large, soft brown eyes of hers. Those eyes are one of the first things you notice about Susan Browning, and she uses them to perfection as the subservient yet strong-willed Pat. Susan is the daughter of a New Jersey dentist, and she was born and raised in The Garden State. Five feet seven inches tall, with long brown hair, Susan is a graduate of Penn State College. She has been acting since 1963, and before moving to Hollywood lived in Princeton, New Jersey. In 1969 she played Nancy Garrison on "Love Is a Many Splendored Thing."

The winner of a Tony Award for her role in *Promises, Promises*, Marion Mercer has conquered stage, television, and movies. She made her film debut with Dustin Hoffman and Mia Farrow in *John and Mary* and recently starred with Shirley Booth on TV in "A Touch of Grace." Unlike her character of Wanda Rittenhouse, Marion is not calculating. She is from Akron, Ohio, and is a graduate of the University of Michigan. Marion has made millions of people laugh in her appearances on television with Johnny Carson, Sandy Duncan, Alan King, Zero Mostel, and Phyllis Diller.

6
The Young and the Restless

Even before the occupants of Genoa City were formed in the mind of creator Bill Bell, he had been approached by all three major networks and Procter & Gamble about developing a new serial. His success with "Days of Our Lives," one of the highest-rated serials, was well known. Finally Bell decided to develop "The Young and the Restless," which has had a remarkable success since it debuted on CBS March 31, 1973.

Bell was discouraged in the embryo stages of his new serial and even considered removing it from the air. About fourteen months after "The Young and the Restless" began, however, it started climbing in the Nielsen ratings; it is now consistently in the top five shows.

Bell, along with his capable assistant Kay Alden, weaves the stories that have captured the large viewing public. Along with dramatic sequences are the factual, informative episodes that have made "The Young and the Restless" so popular, including stories about obesity, mastectomy, and rape.

Chris Brooks was the focal point of the show in its early days. A young, naive college student, she had her sights set on Snapper Foster, a medical student. Chris felt her place in the world would be complete as soon as she married and could start a family.

Chris waited patiently for the day Snapper would ask her to be his wife. She was aware that Snapper felt great responsibility toward his own family—he had helped support them ever since his father disappeared—and she respected his wish to become established before they embarked on a life together.

Happy in her dreams, Chris was crushed when her father, Stuart, told her of Snapper's affair with Sally McGuire. Determined to forget the past, Chris moved out of her family's house and into her own apartment. She went to work for Snapper's brother, Greg, not knowing that her father was subsidizing Greg to pay for her salary.

Once a victim of rape, Chris Foster (Trish Stewart) is now trying to help her little sister, Peggy, cope with the same problem.

Chris enjoyed her freedom, but one night, George Curtis tried to befriend her and raped her. Chris thought her life was over. No longer pure for the man she hoped to marry, she hid herself in her room. But Chris was strong, too; she pressed charges against Curtis. By the time the trial was over, Curtis was set free, and Chris really began to believe she might have enticed Curtis to commit the rape.

Snapper came to the rescue. Both he and Greg had proposed to Chris, hoping to help her realize she was still desirable and had not changed in their eyes. But Chris refused them. Then Curtis was shot by a man when he attempted to rape the man's wife. Snapper managed to get a bedside confession from Curtis and played the tape for Chris.

Chris realized she was not going crazy, and she and Snapper were married. But Chris was not to find the happiness she expected in marriage. When she lost her child, she wanted to go to work and make something of her life. Snapper felt she should stay home and let him struggle to make ends meet. Finally, Chris's gentle persuasion made Snapper realize that she needed more than cleaning the house to keep herself occupied.

Today Snapper and Chris have built their marriage on strong foundations and open communication between them. They are hoping to start a family, knowing the time is now right for such a major step.

The eldest Brooks daughter is Leslie. Frightened of the outside world, feeling plain and without much personality, she buried herself in her music studies, always dreaming of a career as a concert pianist but never believing it would materialize.

Even though her parents encouraged her, Leslie believed that she was in competition with her sister Lorie. When Brad Eliot arrived in Genoa City, Leslie felt completely at ease with him. A former psychologist, Brad realized that Leslie needed gentle prodding, not force, to realize her dreams. With his encouragement, Leslie was able to fulfill her wishes. She began to dream of one day marrying this man and felt that this was more happiness than one person should ask for. Then her sister Lorie returned from Europe and decided Brad was the man she wanted.

Brad had always kept his past life a secret. He did not want to reveal that he was once in medicine, since this was a painful subject to him. But Lorie couldn't let sleeping dogs lie and asked Brad for help with the book she was writing. By snooping, Lorie discovered all about his past and convinced Brad she was the one he should marry.

When Leslie was discovered in a mental institution, it was Brad who helped her back to reality; only then did they realize how much they loved each other. Their wedding was a glorious affair.

Their lives were complete and full until Brad suddenly

asked Leslie for a divorce. Hurt and confused, Leslie didn't want to consent, but she finally decided to agree to the divorce because Brad was so adamant about it. Only after Lorie told Leslie that Brad was almost completely blind did Leslie decide it was time they stopped game playing and tried to make a life for themselves. But Brad was so wrapped up in his self-pity and self-denial that he couldn't see that Leslie was right.

Always wanting the good life, Jill Foster dreamed of mansions and money but was not realistic enough to work for them. When she was given the opportunity to work for wealthy Kay Chancellor, Jill grabbed it, happy to be in the surroundings of wealth, even if it wasn't hers.

Jill fell in love with Phillip Chancellor, Kay's husband, and he returned her feelings. They kept their love a secret until they were sure that Kay, an alcoholic, could stand on her own. But Kay found out about them, and in the end it was she who caused Phillips's death.

Pregnant, Jill had nowhere to turn. Brock Reynolds, Kay's son from a prior marriage, gave Jill a shoulder to lean on and someone to talk to. Brock, a reborn Christian, tried to persuade his mother to give up drink and turn to the Bible. Giving was all that mattered in this world, he said, but no matter how he tried to convince Kay of this, she could only follow her selfish ways.

When Phillip, Jr., was born, Jill tried to claim his part of the estate. Although Brock was on her side, Jill's claim was thrown out of court. An antagonism remains between Jill and Kay, which even Brock is not able to bind into love.

The torment that surrounded Lorie Brooks' life was mostly self-inflicted. Feeling jealous and in the shadow of her talented sister Leslie, Lorie took herself off to Europe for many years. But even this retreat was not what she needed to find solace.

When she returned to Genoa City, she thought Brad Eliot was the man to give her what she wanted. But Brad really loved Leslie. Once again, Lorie felt second-best to her sister.

Then Lorie found Mark Henderson, and they fell deeply in love. Again, love and acceptance were to elude her, for Mark discovered that he and Lorie were fathered by the same man. Mark left Genoa City. Lorie was destroyed, and even though she was usually understanding when it came to affairs of the heart, the circumstances of her parentage put an insurmountable chasm between her and her mother.

Leslie, realizing that she and Lorie must become friends, introduced Lorie to Lance Prentiss. Wealthy and worldly, Lance and Lorie took an immediate dislike to each other. Lance really loved Leslie, but because of her marital status he could not allow himself the luxury of telling Leslie the truth. Eventually Lorie's little-girl ways and provocative life style began to wear Lance down, and he

The bright smile of Brenda Dickson is not often seen in her role of Jill Foster.

The Young and the Restless

asked her to marry him. But Lorie did not realize there was another woman in Lance's life, his mother, Vanessa.

Vanessa had been badly injured in a fire while saving Lance's life. Because of this, she managed to keep Lance tied to her through pity and responsibility. Suffering from a heart ailment, Vanessa was never able to undergo the plastic surgery that would have repaired the damage to her face, and she has lived a life of solitude since the accident.

Disliking Lorie, and feeling that she is not the proper wife for her son, Vanessa has declared war on Lorie and her plans to marry Lance. Not one to take things sitting down, Lorie has taken up the challenge. But Lorie's insecurities about Leslie still lie beneath the surface, and now that Leslie and Brad are divorcing, Lorie wants to rush her marriage to Lance in order to secure her position in his life.

The foundations of the Brooks family were established by Stuart and Jennifer. Married for thirty years, Stuart had no idea that his wife had had an affair with his best friend during a brief separation in their early years together. Jennifer never forgot the man she once almost married and often wondered if he could be the father of Lorie, since Lorie was so different from her other daughters.

With her children grown and self-sufficient, Jennifer decided to leave Stuart and try a life with her former lover, Bruce Henderson. But as the divorce papers were about to be served, Jennifer found a lump on her breast. She left Bruce and returned to Genoa City to be near her family in her time of need.

When the diagnosis turned out to be cancer, Jennifer underwent a mastectomy. Her daughters were there to support her; even Peggy, her youngest, broke down and admitted that she didn't want her mother to die, though she resented her mother's interference in her family situation.

Stuart, too, wanted Jen to come back to him, and in time she did. But Jennifer's secret couldn't be kept forever. Stuart overheard Lorie and Leslie discussing Jennifer's indiscretion, and Stuart saw red. He wanted to throw Jen out of the house, but when the doctors found a heart irregularity in Jennifer during her physical, he changed his mind.

Stuart has kept quiet about his knowledge, but Jennifer can sense an unhappiness in their relationship. Neither wants to endanger or hurt the other. Soft-spoken Jen feels that she has successfully kept her secret and does not want to hurt the man she really loves. Stuart feels helpless in a situation over which he has no control.

The youngest Brooks daugher, Peggy, took her parents' separation very hard. It began to affect her schoolwork, but one of her professors took an interest in Peggy and gave her the attention she so desperately needed at the time. Peggy accepted the aid of

Sexy and sensuous is the only way to describe both Jaime Lyn Bauer and her character, Lorie Brooks Prentiss.

A concerned father for his TV daughters as well as his real-life family is Robert Colbert, who plays Stuart Brooks, newspaper publisher.

34 THE SERIALS

her teacher, which turned into love, and she dreamed of a life with him. She had no idea that Jack Curtis was married. When Stuart found out about the affair from Chris, he immediately went to Peggy. Distraught, Peggy confronted Jack with this information, and he admitted that he was married but that his marriage was unhappy.

Peggy realized that Jack was in a bad situation and stood by him as he tried to untangle his life. His wife, Joann, had become completely dependent on him; she also felt sorry for herself, because she was badly overweight. Peggy told Joann that she would help her to help herself, in order to give Joann a fair chance at winning Jack back.

But before Jack could obtain his divorce, Peggy was raped at her sister Chris's apartment. Peggy went through the same self-doubts that Chris had had, but Peggy had the support of her sisters and Jack.

Peggy's rapist was set free, as the man who raped Chris had been, but Chris decided to trap him. Peggy, needing time to work out things by herself, finally accepted Jack's marriage proposal.

Joann felt deserted, and it was Brock's support that helped her through the dark days of her divorce and made her want to begin living again. Joann realized what her mistakes were and was determined to correct them, knowing that she could not have a happy relationship with any man if she did not mature.

Left:
Trying a new approach to marriage is Peggy Brooks Curtis, who is played by happily married Pamela Solow.

Right:
Watching Joann Curtzinski lose weight on the show has been an inspiration to many viewers. But Kay Heberle, who plays her, will not reveal the diet she followed.

The Young and the Restless

A woman with a wonderful sense of humor is Julianna McCarthy; her portrayal of Liz Foster shows great inner strength.

Snapper Foster (David Hasselhoff) has had his medical career endangered because of his father's death.

Peggy has decided to drop out of school when she and Jack are married in order to help support him. Stuart takes exception to this, feeling Jack will only be using his daughter as he used Joann. And in truth, Peggy is not ready for marriage, but she feels that this is the only way to overcome the fears brought on by her rape.

Liz Foster did the best she could while raising her three children alone. She was both mother and father to them after her husband deserted her, and she is extremely proud of them. When Bill Foster, her husband, returned home after a thirteen-year absence, Liz, son Greg, and daughter Jill welcomed him with open arms. Because Bill had but a short time to live, Liz and he were remarried, and Stuart and Jennifer Brooks gave them a Hawaiian honeymoon.

But, shortly after their return, Bill's illness became much worse. Greg could not accept the fact that a miracle would not happen and that his father would not recover. He refused to listen to his family as they tried to help him accept the truth.

When Bill's illness became so bad that he was in extreme pain, he made Liz remember her promise to let him die a dignified death. Liz, unable to see her husband suffer further, pulled the plug on the machinery that was keeping him alive.

With all the tears Trish Stewart has shed in her role of Chris, you would think she would have permanently red eyes. But Trish's clear blue eyes sparkle with fun and mischief. Recently divorced, she has been having a great time embarking on a new life. The daughter of an army man, Trish traveled a great deal in her early life, and this may have contributed to her open, friendly manner. She tries to keep an even balance between her castmates and is well liked by them.

Taking over the role of Snapper Foster was not easy for David Hasselhoff, but he kept a cool head and listened to the advice given him by the rest of the cast. As this is his first daytime serial, he feels he has learned a lot about acting and is excited at the prospects of learning even more. A bachelor, David has no plans to marry in the near future. Born on July 17 in Baltimore, Maryland, he has a great sense of humor and loves singing, tennis, and any kind of water sport.

After a short time of "treading water," as they say, Tom Hallick is very excited about having a good story to play.

Playing a blind man isn't an easy task for any actor, but Tom Hallick (Brad Eliot) seems to be doing his best to convince the audience of his plight. In real life Hallick's brown eyes see clearly that it is hard work that makes an actor popular and desired. Hallick is devoted to his young daughter, Ashley, and his lady, Pam Crawford. Living near the water, Tom finds it easy to enjoy his interests in water sports and rugged activities such as backpacking and

36 THE SERIALS

camping. An admitted night person, Tom has a great sense of humor and an easy, relaxed manner.

Newly married Brenda Dickson is the perky, bubbly opposite of her trouble-ridden character, Jill. At one time Brenda wanted to be the new Marilyn Monroe, but she has settled down to being a good actress and wife. Concerned about the environment, Brenda encourages her friends to write to people in the government to do something about it. She works hard, and her interests involve gymnastics, dancing, singing, and growing plants. She has begun to enjoy gourmet cooking, something her husband, Robert Rifkin, says she had no interest in before they met.

Surprisingly, Jeanne Cooper takes a motherly attitude toward all the cast members of "The Young and the Restless," something her character Kay Chancellor might want to do but would not allow herself to do. Jeanne's own family is composed of her husband, Harry Berenson, and three children, Collin, Corbin, and Caren. She is very active in local community affairs, especially when they concern children.

Beau Kayzer's rise to stardom has been extraordinary since his debut as Brock. Very interested in the welfare of man, Beau, like Brock, has a strong belief in God. Music is as important to Beau as it is to Brock, and Beau does play the guitar for himself on the show. Serious about his work, Beau enjoys a good joke and has a quick wit. Single, he enjoys playing the field; currently there isn't anyone in sight to take away his bachelor status. His main interest is his new record album.

Left:
Although he plays the blind Brad Eliot on the show, Tom Hallick has eyes for his real-life girl, Pam Crawford.

Right:
Kay Chancellor dotes on her son, Brock Reynolds, and looks to him for support. Jeanne Cooper, who plays Kay, looks upon Beau Kayzer (Brock) as an "adopted son."

The Young and the Restless

In real life John McCook is happily married to Juliet Prowse; his character, Lance Prentiss, has taken the step with Lorie Brooks.

Multi-talented John McCook has found "The Young and the Restless" the best way of showing off his talents without standing in the shadow of his lovely wife, Juliet Prowse. A singer, dancer, and pianist, John has often performed with his wife in Las Vegas, but now, because of his role as Lance Prentiss, he is gratified that people are beginning to recognize him for himself. When Juliet has to leave town to fulfill an engagement, she often takes their young son, Seth, with her. John is a lonely man until his family returns, but he takes these career separations in stride. He has a strong family life and a happy home.

"The Young and the Restless" is not the serial debut for veteran actress K. T. Stevens, who plays the evil, mysterious Vanessa. K. T. is divorced from actor Hugh Marlowe, and has two sons by him, Chris and Jeff. Not one to depend on workmen for repairs, K. T. will build her own extensions onto her house and does most of the interior decorating, sometimes with the help of her sons.

Feeling sorry for her character of Lorie, Jaime Lyn Bauer is also proud of her. Jaime feels Lorie is one of the most interesting characters on the show. Lorie is a survivor, and Jaime is proud of that. She feels, too, that Lorie has evolved to where she is now a full person. The only problem Jaime had in the beginning was her laugh. Lorie was supposed to be bad, but Jaime's laugh changed all that. Perky and vibrant, Jaime is an excellent example of living for today and getting as much out of it as you can. She enjoys dancing, skiing, and horseback riding and has displayed a lovely singing voice on the show.

Although she wears a veil on the show to conceal the face of her character, Vanessa Prentiss, actress K.T. Stevens has no scars to hide, as her son, Chris Marlowe, will attest.

Anxious to make Peggy happy, Jack Curtis (Anthony Herrera) has shown patience with her problem.

38   THE SERIALS

One person who does have control over his life is Robert Colbert, the straightforward, conservative Stuart Brooks. Colbert, the former star of "The Time Tunnel," has found daytime drama to be more difficult than he expected. A veteran of all forms of theater, he is especially proud of his first soap. Colbert and his family—wife, Dorothy, and children, Cami, Shaun, and Clayton Charles—live on the beach in California. He enjoys writing, riding his motorcycle, and building things.

When Dorothy Green (Jennifer Brooks) began on "The Young and the Restless," she was determined not to get involved personally with the other members of the cast. She wanted to keep her relationship strictly on a business level. But the best-laid plans never seem to follow through, and now she feels her TV daughters are as close as her real family. The wife of producer Sidney Miller, Dorothy's own children, Laurel, Jess, and Shelley, are all grown and have lives of their own. She is extremely proud of her four grandchildren. Not one to waste a precious moment of her life, Dorothy is involved in yoga, bike riding, gardening, golf, and taking care of her new home. She's a Capricorn, born on January 12 in Los Angeles.

A private person, Pamela Solow (Peggy Brooks) is married to producer/director Herbert Solow and acquired a ready-made family by her union. This vivacious redhead was born on May 8 in New York and has a multitude of interests that include watercolor painting, the flute, horseback riding, chess, and tennis.

One of Pamela's best friends is Kay Heberle, her arch enemy on the show (Joann). Although Kay was overweight when she joined the show, and had to lose weight for her part, gradually, as Joann began to find herself, in actuality Kay was heavily padded in the beginning. Vivacious Kay, in the middle of dieting, even decided to give up smoking. Burleson, Texas, is home to Kay, and her interests include swimming and playing the piano. Kay met her steady boyfriend when both were in college.

Intense and serious about acting, Anthony Herrera spends most of his time improving his craft. Anthony grew up in Wiggins, Mississippi, but when the acting bug hit, he headed straight for New York. He made his serial debut on "As the World Turns." He also had his own moving business for a while. Now he has a comfortable home along the beaches of Malibu in California. But he still retains his interest in motorcycles.

Strong, independent, and capable is Liz Foster, and so is Julianna McCarthy, who plays her. Julianna has raised her children alone since her divorce from actor Michael Constantine. A person with a good Irish sense of humor, she looks at life carefully, always trying to find the humorous side of it. She will take up challenges and can become very serious when the situation calls for it.

Dorothy Green has a happy home life with her husband, Sidney Miller, but her TV character, Jennifer Brooks, has problems.

The Young and the Restless

Greg Foster's law practice is just starting, as is the career of actor Brian Kerwin.

Newcomer Brian Kerwin was selected after more than a six-month search for Greg Foster. A bachelor, Brian has a steady girl and gets lonely only when she has to be out of town on a job. Before his role as Greg, one of Brian's jobs was as an usher at the famous Grauman's Chinese Theater on Hollywood Boulevard.

40 THE SERIALS

7 All My Children

"All My Children" was the first daytime serial geared specifically toward a college-age viewing audience. But since its January 6, 1970 debut, the show's mature and intelligent handling of serious subjects such as child abuse, abortion, cosmetic surgery, and prostitution has attracted a nationwide audience as diverse as the people who share such dilemmas.

The story line revolves around two families: the Martins and the Tylers. The setting is the fictionalized East Coast town of Pine Valley.

Heading the Martin clan are Dr. Joseph Martin and his wife, Ruth. While both have been featured since the serial's debut, they were not married at the outset of the show. At that time, Ruth Brent, not a wealthy woman, was a person whose kindness and integrity made her friendship a priceless commodity. Her life centered around her husband, Ted, and her teen-aged son, Philip. But a desire to help others enabled her to juggle a happy home life with a fulfilling nursing career. She suffered a great loss when Ted was killed in an automobile crash but eventually overcame her grief as she realized she must go on living.

Dr. Joseph Martin was a conservative, family-oriented man, who had long been a widower. Strict devotion to his career and the responsibility of raising a son, Jeff, and a daughter, Tara, had prevented him from actively pursuing romance.

After Ruth was suddenly widowed, she and Joe realized that their similar backgrounds and grass-roots foundations meshed perfectly. Their long-time friendship turned into love, and they wed.

Deliriously happy, each fulfilled the other's need for security and family. They had worked hard to instill a sense of values in their respective children. But problems in their relationship arose when parental concern turned into meddling.

The three young adults who inadvertently caused the rift between Joe and Ruth Martin are Tara Martin Tyler, Philip Brent, and Chuck Tyler. All have been friends since childhood, and while Tara and Phil were raised in modest surroundings, Chuck is from one of Pine Valley's wealthiest families. Only his humility and essentially kind disposition prevent him from using family influence or wealth to his own advantage.

Phil and Chuck had one common interest: Tara. But it was never a contest, for Tara and Phil shared an idealistic young love and whiled away hours composing their own love songs and dreaming of a future together. Tara's strict upbringing, reflected in her modest demeanor and high moral standards, was an integral part of her, which Philip respected.

Their idyllic existence faced a large dose of reality when Philip discovered that he was not the biological son of his parents; he had been adopted at birth by Ruth and Ted but was the child of Ruth's unmarried sister, Amy, and her lover, Nick Davis. Believing himself badly deceived, Philip fled to New York. Deeply questioning his own identity, he felt unworthy to share his life with anyone. His letters to Tara dwindled, then stopped.

Unaware of his emotional state, a brokenhearted Tara became involved with Chuck. But Philip could not forget his family and friends and eventually returned to Pine Valley, where he was reconciled with Tara.

When Phil received his draft notice, he and Tara decided to marry immediately. Unaware of how to locate the proper legal authorities, the young lovers stole away and conducted their own private ceremony, exchanging vows that they had written themselves.

Philip was sent to Vietnam. And at the same time that Tara received confirmation of her pregnancy, she learned that Philip was reported killed. Morally unable to abort the child, she related her problems to a sympathetic Chuck. He immediately proposed marriage. Not only did he truly want to be the father of her as yet unborn child, but Chuck had long been deeply in love with Tara. His understanding and compassion swayed her, and they were married. They named their son Philip Tyler.

After the baby was born, news arrived of Philip Brent's survival. Tara's love for him had never died, but she tried to keep her marriage intact for the sake of the child.

Philip, on the rebound, married seductive Erica Kane Martin. But when he discovered that Tara's baby was his biological son, he no longer saw any reason for being parted from Tara.

Tara and Philip divorced their respective spouses, and for a time their future looked bright. But Philip was unable to secure employment for a long while and his self-esteem suffered. Further strain was caused by Tara's guilt over separating Chuck from the

The original Tara, who has played the role twice since its inception, was Karen Gorney.

baby Philip and Chuck's subsequent involvement with former prostitute Donna Beck.

Chuck Tyler had been raised by his grandparents and obtained his sense of fair play and compassionate nature from his marvelous, down-to-earth grandfather, Dr. Charles Tyler. His stepgrandmother, Phoebe, has always made it abundantly clear to everyone that the Tylers of Pine Valley are an important family and one to be reckoned with!

Phoebe deeply loves her son, Lincoln, her daughter, Anne, and her grandson, Chuck, but her definition of maternal concern is translated by others as blatant interference into their personal affairs. Although Phoebe's world revolves around the children's personal happiness, to her, the word happiness means social stature and financial security. Much to Phoebe's dismay, the other Tylers look beyond appearances and bank statements to a person's true worth.

Charles has suffered humiliation silently during his long marriage. He escaped Phoebe's incessant bickering by devoting himself to his work as hospital chief-of-staff, but his home life became intolerable as his friendship with secretary Mona Kane deep-

Dr. Charles Tyler (that's Hugh Franklin on the left) has been in love with his secretary, Mona Kane (Fra Heflin), with the approval of his son, Lincoln (Peter White).

All My Children 43

ened into a lovely, warm relationship. Now that Charles has found the companionship that has eluded him for so long, he has asked Phoebe for a divorce in order to marry Mona.

Phoebe was incensed at the divorce request. Not only did she refuse to relinquish the status of being Mrs. Charles Tyler II, but she also would not suffer the humiliation of losing Charles to a lower-class "homewrecker" like Mona Kane!

Dr. Tyler's good qualities have been passed on to his daughter, Anne, whom he adores. Unable to confide in or trust her mother, Anne and her father have long shared a close relationship.

Anne is a passionate, highly emotional person. Whether in a business venture or a love affair, she immerses herself in an undertaking with uncommon dedication. A startlingly attractive woman, the adolescent Anne seemed to have everything; she went to all the "right" schools; owned a wardrobe stocked with the latest fashions, and had gracious manners. But none of this could give her the one thing she desperately wanted: personal happiness. In marrying free spirit Nick Davis, she seemed to find the deep love and devotion that had eluded her for so long.

The union appalled Phoebe, who felt that Nick was beneath Anne's notice and poor husband material as well. But Anne's heart told her it was right. The only thing she needed to make life complete was a child.

Although born on the wrong side of the tracks, Nick was an intensely proud man. Determined not to touch a penny of his wife's money, he swore to support her in a manner equal to her Tyler heritage.

Nick's male ego plummeted when he learned from doctors that his sperm count was low. Chances were great that he would never be able to father a child. Believing that he could not give Anne the one thing she truly desired, Nick decided to ask Anne for a divorce. But he would not tell her the real reason. Their final night together resulted in Anne's pregnancy. But she refused to tell him about the child because she thought he would stay with her only out of a sense of duty.

Handsome, successful lawyer Paul Martin had long been in love with Anne. When he learned of her condition, he begged her to let him be a husband to her and father to her child. She hesitated, telling him that she was not in love with him, but Paul's persistence paid off, and she finally relented and married him.

After Anne suffered a miscarriage, the marriage deteriorated. Paul was a patient man and tried to give Anne time to sort out her feelings. She had discovered the true reason Nick had divorced her and tried to hate him. But their passion was still very much alive.

Paul's pride could no longer tolerate such abuse. Dis-

The gracious Anne Tyler Martin (Judith Barcroft) became obsessed with the well-being of her retarded daughter, Beth.

44 THE SERIALS

Paul Martin (William Mooney) has tried to ease his wife's anxieties about their baby, but Anne (Judith Barcroft) has made it extremely difficult.

liking the jealous, suspicious man he was turning into, he agreed to a divorce.

Only much later did Anne realize that her love for Nick had turned into no more than friendship. Love plays inexplicable games with the heart, and Anne found herself deeply in love with Paul. He, too, admitted that he had never stopped loving her. Not only had they been given a second opportunity at marriage, but their prayers had been answered. Anne discovered herself pregnant.

Anne became ill, and the diagnosis was a rare blood disorder. The doctors suggested an abortion because her illness could affect the fetus. But believing in the quality of every life, Anne refused even to consider the alternative.

When her daughter, Elizabeth, was born, she looked beautiful and healthy. But preliminary tests performed by pediatrician Dr. Christina Karras disclosed that the baby had indeed been afflicted with the blood disorder. Because they will not know the extent of the child's illness until she reaches adolescence, Anne and Paul must take things a day at a time.

Dr. Christina Karras's professional career is proceeding nicely, but her personal life has not proved as successful. One of the men in her past was Dr. David Thornton. Their affair in San Fran-

All My Children 45

A woman with a secretive past is Dr. Christina Karras (Robin Strasser).

cisco came to a mutual halt, but now that both reside in Pine Valley, old sentiments have been stirred.

Phoebe Tyler was taken aback by son Lincoln's choice of a wife, Kitty Shea Davis. Because Kitty had two unsuccessful marriages behind her and a questionable past, Phoebe did everything in her power to try to break up the match. Kitty, herself, felt that Lincoln deserved a better wife, but his devotion and love eventually won her over. Phoebe's pompous manner made her unable to see what a warm, kind woman Kitty was.

When Kitty's first husband returned to Pine Valley, he revealed that their divorce had never been legally finalized; her marriage to Linc was annulled. After her divorce, Linc begged her to remarry him, but she decided that he would be better off without her.

To insure their separation, Phoebe hired a woman to pose as Kitty's long-lost mother and create further strain in Kitty and Lincoln's relationship. The plan backfired, as Kitty's "assigned mother" grew to love her new daughter and devised a plan to stage her own death and funeral, thus exiting from Kitty's life as painlessly as possible. After this episode, Kitty and Lincoln decided to remarry.

Mary Fickett's sensitive and convincing portrayal of Ruth Martin has been so successful that it won her the first daytime Emmy Award as best leading actress in 1973. A veteran of many theatrical and television productions, Mary has portrayed Ruth Martin since "All My Children" made its debut. She has been married to actor James Congdon and businessman Len Scheer, but is now single. Truly optimistic about her life, she is blessed with a keen wit and a sharp sense of humor, and her warm personality makes her a total joy.

Of his characterization as Dr. Joseph Martin, actor Ray MacDonnell comments, "I could use a little bit more excitement. He [Joe] is awfully good and awfully straight! I've been so virtuous!" Needless to say, Ray possesses a dry humor. In fact, during early morning rehearsals on the set, it's a laugh a minute when he and Mary get together. But, like Joe Martin, Ray is an intensely private man, who jealously guards the home life he shares with his wife, Joan, and their children, Kyle, Sara, and Daniel, in their upstate New York home.

The character of Philip is portrayed by Nick Benedict. He is regarded as an eligible bachelor by the ladies—and also by himself! Currently divorced, he has definitely not soured on matrimony and yearns for the day when he'll meet the right woman and be able to share his life and raise a family. In the meantime, the actor busies himself playing drums in various local nightclub engagements and escapes New York City on weekends by traveling upstate on his motorcycle. Of his character on the serial, Nick com-

Happily reunited are Linc Tyler (Peter White) and Kitty Shea (Francesca James). But for how long?

Because her adopted son was fathered by Nick Davis (Larry Keith), Ruth Martin (Mary Fickett) has kept up a cordial, and sometimes friendly, relationship with him.

All My Children 47

Dr. Joseph Martin (Ray MacDonnell) is often headstrong and stubborn, to his own detriment.

Phil Brent (Nick Benedict) went through some shattering experiences in his youth.

ments, "I think the writers should make him a little looser . . . let him have more fun."

Although Nancy Frangione now plays the part of Tara Martin Tyler Brent, many "All My Children" fans will always remember Karen Gorney, who originated the role. She left after two years (in 1972) to try a singing and acting career in Hollywood. In early 1975, she returned to portray Tara once again. In her absence, she'd noticed the increased sophistication of the serials, and at long last, they were being regarded as a true art form. Divorced from Ken Golden, Karen lives on Manhattan's Upper West Side. She composes music and often accompanies herself on guitar and performs in various clubs around the city.

Although handsome Richard Van Vleet (who likes to be called "Van") is the third actor to play the role of Chuck Tyler, without a doubt he's the most popular to date! A native of Denver, Colorado, when he won the role on this serial he was living in California with his wife, Kristin, and daughters, Shannon and Heather. A devoted family man, he says he went through some lonely moments until the three women in his life could join him. The Van Vleets now live in suburban New Jersey.

48 THE SERIALS

The role of Erica Brent is convincingly played by actress Susan Lucci, a beautiful brunette who considers her role as mother to three-year-old Lisa as the number-one role in her life. Susan's husband, Helmut Huber, was born in Austria. At least once a year, they try to return to his homeland for their favorite pastime, skiing.

"He's too good!" So says Hugh Franklin of his character, Dr. Charles Tyler. This fine veteran of numerous Broadway productions would not stand for a nagging wife like Phoebe in real life because he is married to talented author Madeleine L'Engle. They reside in Manhattan and are very close to their three children and two grandchildren. A completely liberated husband, Hugh enjoys stepping into the kitchen and whipping up some culinary delight!

Prior to her Phoebe Tyler role, Ruth Warrick was an accomplished star of the Broadway stage (*Irene*) and Hollywood screen (*Citizen Kane*). Currently separated from her husband, Jarvis Cushing, this super-talent recently entered yet another phase of her multifaceted career: her own nightclub act. When asked if she resembled Phoebe, Ruth replied seriously, "I think my tongue can take care of people pretty well when I get angry, but I don't do it often." She then jokingly added, "Mostly, I'm a dear, sweet, loving person!"

Although many husbands and wives find it hard to work together on a project, the serial's Anne Tyler Martin, Judith Barcroft, and her husband, "All My Children" writer Wisner Washam, say just the opposite is true! Judith says that in no way were they in competition; he outlined scripts a month before she performed them. And she somehow refrained from inquiring about her character's fate. "So many people are always asking me what's going to happen. I'm afraid if I really knew, I might inadvertently let it slip!" A devoted couple, Judith and Wisner are happiest when spending time with Ian, five, and Amy, three. Unlike many other young couples, the Washams adore living in New York City and find it a very creative environment in which to raise children.

Like his character, Nick Davis, actor Larry Keith is now single and likes it that way! There are two special ladies in his life: his daughter, Lisa, who attends Ithaca College, and his girl friend. Larry is an avid pilot who flys his own Cessna plane. And the next time you see a television commercial, if Larry's not visible, listen carefully: he's probably doing the voice-over!

Paul Martin is portrayed by Bill Mooney. He and his lovely wife, opera singer Valerie Goodall, are the parents of twin sons, Will and Sean, and reside in suburban New Jersey. The actor considers his work a hobby; he enjoys playing Mr. Fixit around the house.

Actress Robin Strasser made a welcome return to the day-

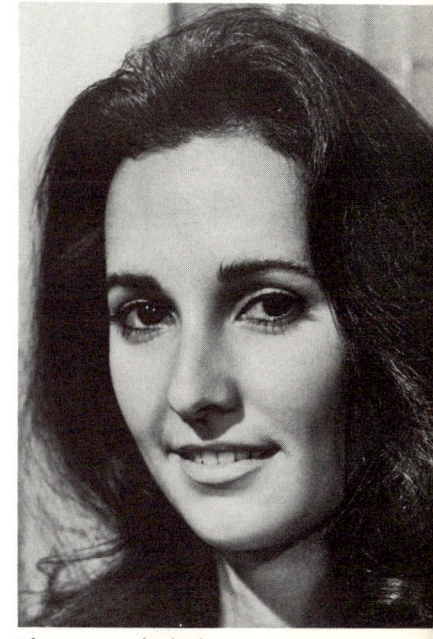

The sex symbol of Pine Valley, Erica Brent, is played by lovely Susan Lucci.

Phoebe Tyler (Ruth Warrick) is very much aware of her social status, but lately she has been hitting the bottle.

All My Children 49

time scene when she created the role of Dr. Christina Karras. Previously, she had played villainess Rachel Davis Frame on "Another World" for six years. Robin and her husband, actor Laurence Luckinbill, are the parents of two sons, Benjamin and Joseph, and reside on Manhattan's Upper East Side.

Lincoln Tyler is portrayed by actor Peter White. Besides starring in the movie *Boys in the Band,* Peter has appeared in numerous Broadway and nighttime TV roles. He's a bachelor and resides in Manhattan.

Francesca James is a woman of many talents. In addition to appearing in her Kitty Tyler role, last year she made her operatic debut singing lieder at Manhattan's Alice Tully Hall. She's a firm devotee of mind control. She's also single, and lives in New York City.

8
One Life to Live

The fictionalized East Coast town of Llanview is the locale for the popular ABC serial "One Life to Live." The serial debuted on July 15, 1968, and has increased its audience annually, to the point where today Nielsen ratings consistently place it in the top five daytime serials.

On July 26, 1975, ABC expanded the half-hour serial to forty-five minutes. The increased time allowance and larger cast have added to the show's reputation as a highly informative, educational daytime serial. Especially commendable are the serial's true-to-life portrayals. For example, when the drama dealt with narcotics, location scenes were shot at New York's Odyssey House, a drug rehabilitation center, and addicts were cast in several roles.

In the serial Dr. Jim Craig and his wife, Anna, are a pleasant, down-to-earth couple who provide needed stability in their troubled friends' lives. Their comfortable existence and strong moral values are often a source of envy even among their wealthier friends. Although neither Jim nor Anna holds an unrealistic view of life, whenever the world appears to be closing in, they can turn to each other for strength and love.

Jim's daughter from a previous marriage, Cathy, has been a source of much worry and concern. Highly independent and in constant search for the new and untried, Cathy became involved with drugs as a teen-ager and almost ruined her life. Seeking a career as an author, she seemed finally to have found her niche in life. But an affair with newspaperman Joe Riley resulted in her pregnancy, and knowing that Joe did not love her, she refused his marriage proposal and opted to have the child out of wedlock. Cathy adored her daughter, Megan, but when the baby died of a heart malfunction, Cathy once again felt empty and alone.

Llanview newcomer Tony Lord, the illegitimate son of wealthy newspaper publisher Victor Lord, became romantically involved with Cathy. Independent and brash, Tony had played at romance until he met Cathy. For the first time, he wanted the security and responsibility of marriage. But Cathy did not believe that they needed a wedding certificate to make their love legal.

Because she refused his proposal, Cathy and Tony went their separate ways. But another female had her eye on Tony. Patricia Kendall had known Tony ten years earlier, when both were employed in South America. They had been lovers, but when she wanted marriage, he had left her.

Pat, an intelligent, career-minded woman, nevertheless yearned for a stable home life and someone with whom to share her life. Not long after she and Tony parted, she discovered that she was pregnant. Pride prevented her from informing Tony of her condition. Instead, she quickly married Paul Kendall, who promised to be a father to her child because he loved her. But her husband was wanted by federal authorities on suspicion of illegal bombings, and soon after her arrival in Llanview, he was reported killed in a fire.

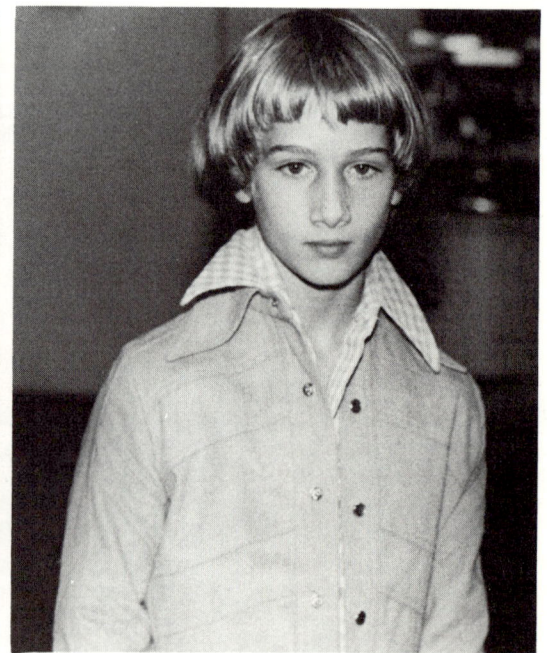

Left:
Pat Kendall (Jacquie Courtney) has kept the secret of her son's parentage for years.

Right:
Brian Kendall (Steven Austin) is an average kid who loves sports.

Pat planned to tell Tony that Brian was his son, but Cathy discovered this fact first and quickly reconciled with Tony. She told him that she had reconsidered and desperately wanted to marry him. Cathy then became obsessed with having a child of her own.

Although Victoria Lord Riley was the daughter of one of Llanview's first families, she has always been careful not to let her money or upper-class background interfere with her relationships with people. She fell in love with Joe Riley, a boy from the wrong side of the tracks who made good. At first, Viki's father objected to the match, but Joe's determination and honesty eventually won Victor over.

52   THE SERIALS

Joe desperately wanted to have a family and could not understand why his wife was so reluctant to have children. Joe was unaware that he had a hereditary heart ailment, a fact that Viki alone knew. In all probability, this condition would be inherited by any child that Joe fathered. Joe and Cathy's daughter, Megan, who had been conceived before Joe and Viki were married, had the ailment and suffered an attack when Viki was minding her. In Viki's subsequent rush to the hospital she had an accident, and Megan died before she reached medical attention. Cathy accused Viki of killing her child, and although Joe insisted the death was not Viki's fault, Viki could not rid herself of guilt.

Afraid that the truth about his heart would hurt Joe, Viki decided not to tell him about it but to become pregnant and risk the chance that their baby would not inherit Joe's disease. Although it was a long, tedious pregnancy, Viki gave birth to a perfectly healthy son, Kevin.

Later, Joe and Cathy inadvertently discovered the true nature of Megan's heart condition. While Joe eventually forgave Viki for concealing the truth, Cathy withdrew into herself, convinced that she could trust no one. Jealous of Viki's healthy baby, Cathy kidnapped Kevin from the hospital. Joe and Viki, frantic, spared no expense hunting down clues to the whereabouts of Cathy and Kevin.

His wife's erratic behavior convinces Tony that he never really knew Cathy. He now realizes that theirs has been no more than a physical attraction and that the woman he truly loves is Pat Kendall.

Viki's mother died when she was just a child, and she had often wished that her father, Victor, would find another woman to love and make his life complete. But she had great trouble understanding his selection of Dr. Dorian Cramer, a sly, devious woman, who never made an uncalculated move in her life.

Victor and Dorian met in the hospital where Victor was recuperating from a heart attack. He knew of Dorian's reputation but believed that others had not seen the side of her personality that he knew—seemingly warm, unselfish, and strong in her concern for others.

After their marriage, Dorian's dream of living in the Lord mansion was at last realized. But when Victor discovered that Dorian had tried to hide the existence of his illegitimate son, Tony Lord, they argued bitterly. Victor suffered a heart attack and died.

Anna Craig and her brothers, Larry and Vincent, are extremely close. After Larry Wolek's beloved wife Meredith died, he divided his time between raising their son, Danny, and his successful medical career. But his attractive second cousin, Karen, came to town and decided to show Larry all the finer things that life had to

Lee Patterson is smiling but as Joe Riley he is too upset over the disappearance of his child to concentrate on his work.

One Life to Live 53

The marriage of Larry Wolek (Michael Storm) and Karen Wolek (Kathy Breech) has gone up in smoke, but for how long?

offer. Larry had been without a woman for so long that he quickly succumbed to Karen's physical attractiveness and vivacious youth. Much to Anna and Vince's displeasure, Larry and Karen became engaged.

Ambitious and underhanded, Karen felt that marriage to a doctor would afford her a comfortable life style. Larry's grass-roots upbringing and unpretentious ways did not mesh with Karen's dreams, but she had high hopes of changing him into the kind of man she wanted.

Karen and her sister, Jenny, are opposites. Jenny had been a nun but left the sisterhood to marry Tim Siegel. Even after his death, she retained her deep religious convictions and strict moral code.

Jenny's warmth and humility have attracted two admirers: tennis pro Brad Vernon and his psychiatrist father, Dr. Will Vernon. Brad, used to winning any female's affection he tried for, was intrigued by Jenny's resistance and shy nature. His father has long endured an unhappy marriage to Naomi. Because of a love affair Will had many years ago, Naomi no longer trusts him and fre-

54   THE SERIALS

quently accuses him of affairs with an assortment of young women. Will's eyes had never wandered after that affair, until he met Jenny, however.

No matter how hard he tries, Larry and Anna's brother, Vinnie always manages to bungle things. His loving wife, Wanda, constantly warns him to stay out of other people's affairs, but Vinnie's love and concern for his family always causes him to intervene. There's been some rough going in Vinnie and Wanda's marriage, but their mutual devotion and good humor have gotten them through the hardest of times. Recently Vinnie, a bit of a male chauvinist, complained when Wanda went to work, but as usual, she won the day by letting him think he had triumphed in the argument.

Dr. Jim Craig is portrayed by Nat Polen. Playing the role of a father comes naturally to him, as he has three daughters of his own. An introspective, thoughtful man, Nat is philosophical about life and a very interesting conversationalist. He and his wife, Ruth, live in upstate New York. To relax, Nat enjoys playing golf and spending time with his two grandchildren. Before becoming an actor, he was a professional jazz drummer.

Kathleen Maguire has now brought her own special style to the role of Anna Craig, but Doris Belack gave it the touch of a

Well-meaning but often interfering is Vinnie Wolek (here played by Jordan Charney).

Patience is the major virtue of Dr. Jim Craig, played by Nat Polen.

One Life to Live 55

talented comedienne. Although she enjoyed her role on the show, Doris worried that her character was too good to be true. "Always inviting friends to stay for dinner," Doris jokes, "Anna's got the A & P freezer in her kitchen!" In her personal life, Doris is happily married to Broadway producer Philip Rose and frequently appears in stage productions. The couple live in an elegant Manhattan apartment, and unlike Anna, Doris hates to cook, sew, knit, or clean house. The Roses have no children, but they have two pets: a poodle, named Crazy Louie, and a Labrador, named Suzie.

Cathy Lord is convincingly portrayed by Jennifer Harmon. Independent and free-spirited, she is a firm believer in equal rights for women. Jennifer is divorced and lives on Manhattan's Upper West Side. Her constant companion for the past few years has been actor Ken Kerchival. To relax, she enjoys sewing, hunting for antiques, and yoga.

Discovering his mistake in marrying Cathy Craig (Jennifer Harmon), Tony Lord (George Reinholt) has no way of getting out of the union.

Now that Philip MacHale has taken over the role of Tony Lord, George Reinholt has gone on to exercise his many other talents. He plays a mean piano, has recorded an album, and writes poetry; he hopes to publish a book of poems soon. Bachelor George is consumed by his career and frequently appears in off-Broadway productions. He lives in a co-op in Greenwich Village.

It is a shame that her role of Patricia Kendall does not allow Jacqueline Courtney to display her talent for comedy, for this actress possesses a sharp wit and a quick mind. She is presently separated from her husband, Dr. Carl Desiderio, and they have a six-year-old daughter, Jennifer Kristin. Jacquie's ability to laugh at herself is a delight, although she makes no bones about her strong aversion to any kind of housework!

Victoria Lord Riley is played by Erika Slezak, daughter of famed screen actor Walter Slezak. Tired of renting a Manhattan apartment, she bought her own co-op in the city and has been taking her time refurbishing it. Divorced several years ago, Erika says she would try marriage again. A highly likely candidate is fellow actor Brian Davies; Erika met him when both appeared in an off-Broadway play.

One individual who says he doubts that he will ever marry is Lee Patterson, who portrays Joe Riley. A confirmed bachelor, Lee's attitude is "live for today." He makes decisions on the spur of the moment and doesn't like to plan. Still remembered for his starring role in the early 1960s TV hit "Surfside Six," Lee's number-one passion is his boat, *The Moonfleet*. He's studied in-depth navigation and one day hopes to sail solo across the Atlantic Ocean.

Dr. Dorian Lord (now played by Claire Malis) was formerly played by Nancy Pinkerton—bright, energetic, and always on the go! Nancy is a firm advocate of women's rights. Divorced, she lives in a spacious apartment on Manhattan's Upper West Side but spends all her spare time at her country house in upstate New York, where she grows her own vegetables and herbs.

Dr. Larry Wolek is played by Michael Storm. Blonde, hazel-eyed Michael is delightfully unaffected by his fame and considers his first priority his lovely family, to whom he's totally devoted. He and his wife, Sally, and their children, Jason and Maggie, live in a sprawling house in upstate New York. Michael enjoys theater work and often appears in off-Broadway productions.

Kathryn Breech's role as Karen Wolek marked her television debut. Devoted to her career, she makes sure to take sufficient time out to partake of her favorite pastime, horseback riding. She's single, with no immediate plans for marriage, and lives alone in Manhattan.

Jenny Siegel is played by actress Katherine Glass. A firm advocate of the Women's Liberation Movement, she refers to herself as determined. Once she latches onto something, she never lets go. Katherine's been married for a year to stage manager Ted Harris. They reside in Greenwich Village but hope to buy a country house in Pennsylvania or Connecticut.

The character of Brad Vernon is played by Jameson Parker, a young actor totally dedicated to his craft. Because his father was a career officer with the U.S. State Department, Jameson attended schools in such varied locations as West Germany and Swit-

Believing that her son is all right, Viki Riley (Erika Slezak) has been trying to comfort her husband.

Would Dorian Lord (Nancy Pinkerton) really like to steal Joe away from Viki? You bet!

One Life to Live 57

Top left:
Petite Kathryn Breech has been enjoying her role as Karen Wolek.

Top right:
At one time Jenny Wolek (Katherine Glass) was studying to be a nun. Then she met Timmy Siegel, who changed her life.

Bottom right:
After a long movie career, Farley Granger took on the role of Dr. Will Vernon while living in New York and looking for Broadway properties.

58 THE SERIALS

zerland. Jameson now lives in Manhattan with his bride of less than a year, actress Bonnie Parker.

Veteran actor Tony George has taken the part of psychiatrist Will Vernon over from another veteran actor, Farley Granger, who added another dimension to his illustrious career when he joined this serial. His career began at the tender age of fourteen, when he was signed to a movie contract at MGM. He is single and lives in New York City.

Naomi Vernon was portrayed by Teri Keane, easily recognized by daytime audiences from her long-running role on "The Edge of Night" as Martha Marceau. Teri has also been on "As the World Turns" and "Young Dr. Malone." Married to the late actor John Larken, she has a daughter, Sharon, who aspires to follow in her theatrical mother's footsteps.

Vinnie Wolek was expertly played by Jordan Charney, a firm beliver in the occult and ESP. Charney is co-founder of the Dream Healing Theater, a group that analyzes people's dreams. He has been happily married for eleven years to Nancy and they have two children, Allison and Daniel. The Charneys divide their time between a Manhattan apartment and a summer house on Fire Island.

Although Teri Keane looks nice and normal at home in the kitchen, her character, Naomi Vernon, was a neurotic.

One Life to Live 59

9 Days of Our Lives

"Days of Our Lives" debuted November 19, 1965, on NBC and is one of only three serials to be taped on the West Coast. Its high audience ratings over the years enabled it, on April 21, 1975, to become the second hour-long daytime drama. The expanded show's cast is now over forty-five, the largest group on daytime TV. "Days of Our Lives" stresses fine acting, and its innovative writing has produced stories on such controversial topics as artificial insemination and interracial romance.

The major story line surrounds the trials and tribulations of the Horton family and their friends, who all reside in the town of Salem.

Dr. Tom Horton and his wife, Alice, are concerned parents who have long taken an active interest in their children's welfare. While Tom has a successful medical career, he has never let his profession take precedence over the responsibilities of child rearing that he shares with Alice, an emotional, God-fearing woman whose existence revolves around her family. Their children are sons Bill, Mickey, and Tom, Jr., and a daughter, Marie.

Two of the Horton boys, Bill and Mickey, are successful in their professions. Their personal lives, however, leave much to be desired. Both are family-conscious, but Mickey has the more outgoing nature.

A successful criminal lawyer, Mickey was married to Dr. Laura Horton, a psychiatrist, who seemed a rare combination of beauty and brains. She was the envy of many, seemingly able to juggle her career and her home life with ease. But much of her life with Mickey was a living hell. She was laden with guilt, having lived a lie for many years. Unbeknownst to her husband, their son, Mike, was the biological son of Bill Horton.

Shortly after Mickey and Laura wed, Bill raped Laura. That

single encounter produced Mike. Knowing how close Mickey was to his brother, and knowing also (though Mickey was unaware of this) that her husband was sterile and Mike would be their only child, Laura remained silent. Over the years, she actually fell in love with Bill. Tensions mounted, and eventually Mickey and Laura were divorced.

Mickey's problems were just beginning. He suffered a heart attack that left him with amnesia. Unable to recall his identity, he left Salem and began life anew under the name of Marty Hanson. His loneliness was soon eased by a pretty farm girl, Maggie. They fell in love, and once Maggie convinced him that only the future mattered, they married.

Back in Salem, Bill and Laura's dreams finally seemed to be coming true. They were married and a short time later had a daughter, Jennifer Rose.

When "Marty's" memory returned, he and Maggie returned to Salem. Mickey had enough trouble relating to reality, but upon discovering the truth about his son's parentage, he withdrew completely. The cool, calm attorney turned into a pathetic recluse and suffered a mental breakdown.

He was institutionalized and, months later, released against the good advice of his doctor, Marlena Evans. Maggie swore to wait patiently for her husband, until he could come to her of his own free will and out of love. But Linda Patterson, Mickey's former secretary and the woman with whom he had an affair, is still waiting in the background.

"Days of Our Lives" viewers breathed a sigh of relief when long-time lovers Julie Banning Anderson and Doug Williams finally tied the knot after years of sharing undying passion. Their common concern for everyone's feelings but their own had previously prevented them from sharing true happiness.

If dark, shapely, seductive Julie was ever without a man it was by choice, not from lack of attention from the opposite sex. Julie's wry sense of humor and deep love for her family aided her in overcoming disastrous marriages to Scott Banning and Bob Anderson. Following her second divorce, Julie agonized over the fact that she had never married for love.

When Doug arrived in Salem, he was a real lady's man: suave, debonair, smooth-talking. Feeling no sense of responsibility to anyone but himself, he entered into relationships with a variety of women. But Julie demanded his full-time interest, which he rendered. Frustrated at their inability to secure a future together, on the rebound Doug accepted a marriage proposal from Julie's young mother, Addie.

Addie accepted the fact that Doug did not love her, no matter how little he was able to resist her goodness and unselfish

Finally happily married after years of separation are Bill and Laura Horton (Edward Mallory and Rosemary Forsyth).

Days of Our Lives 61

motives. He began to feel closer to her than any woman in his past except Julie. Addie bought Doug his own nightclub, Doug's Place.

At the same time that Addie discovered that she was pregnant, she was tragically stricken with leukemia. But she refused medical assistance until after the birth of her daughter, Hope. Just as things looked bright once more, Addie was struck by a car and killed. But life with Addie had mellowed Doug; he now appreciated true love and realized how rare it really was.

Julie's marriage to an older man, wealthy Bob Anderson, proved unwise from the beginning. While she admired him as a person, she could not love him as a man. Their divorce was amiable.

Following years of heartache, Julie and Doug became engaged—to other people! She agreed to marry her long-time suitor, lawyer Don Craig. Don was handsome, worldly, and possessed a keen wit. Long in love with Julie, Don had almost gotten her to the altar between her first and second marriages. Unable to forget her, he proposed again, and to his shocked delight, she accepted. For his part, Doug, on the rebound, proposed to his ex-wife, a sultry Polynesian beauty named Kim. But fate intervened and prevented Doug and Julie from proceeding with these marital mismatches.

Not so ironically, both couples had selected the same wedding days. The night before the scheduled marriages, Doug was severely injured in an automobile crash. Lying unconscious in the hospital, he could only murmur Julie's name. Coming so close to losing him made Julie realize their love had never died. Following his recuperation, they married and honeymooned in Italy.

Although Kim still regrets losing Doug, Don has been caught on the rebound by the lovely and independent Dr. Marlena Evans, Mickey Horton's analyst.

Julie Williams is not the only female in Salem to know the meaning of anguish. Her close friend, beautiful Amanda Howard, has endured one tragedy after another! Soft-spoken and sensitive, Amanda had long yearned to find the special man with whom she could share her life. Her dreams appeared to come true in Dr. Neil Curtis.

A highly educated man, Neil was physically healthy but suffered from a serious illness: an addiction to gambling. Amanda was aware of this but was convinced that her love would prove a cure-all.

The night before their wedding, Amanda paid an unannounced call on her fiancé, only to find him in the arms of another woman. In a near-hysterical state, she contemplated suicide but was rescued by Dr. Greg Peters. Greg could understand Amanda, for he was recovering from a disastrous first marriage.

The long-awaited marriage of Julie and Doug Williams occurred in October 1976, but real-life husband and wife Bill Hayes and Susan Seaforth Hayes had married some time before.

Although Neil Curtis doesn't have music in his life, Joe Gallison makes his own.

Greg soon fell in love with Amanda, but she was unable to forget Neil.

His gambling got Neil deeply in debt. Believing Amanda was now beyond his grasp, he romanced and married an older wealthy divorcee, Phyllis Anderson, whom Bob had divorced for Julie.

Amanda, meanwhile, suffered further tragedy. She discovered that she had a brain tumor, the same affliction that had taken her mother's life. Both Neil and Greg stood by her and offered emotional support throughout her ordeal. But just as it looked as if Amanda and Neil would reconcile, Phyllis announced that she was pregnant. Amanda refused to see any more of Neil and accepted Greg's proposal of marriage. They married shortly thereafter.

Dr. Tom Horton is played by veteran star of stage and screen, Macdonald Carey, who received the daytime Emmy Award as best actor in 1972, 1973, and 1974. Mac lives in Beverly Hills, California, and is a tennis fanatic, finding in tennis a great form of exercise and a tension reliever. In his thirty years in show business, Mac has appeared in more than fifty films. He was divorced several years ago but remains close to his six children. He is a member of the Board of the Motion Picture Academy and also active in the Catholic Big Brothers Organization.

Days of Our Lives 63

Executive producer Betty Corday with her stars, Macdonald Carey (Dr. Tom Horton) and Frances Reid (Alice Horton).

Frances Reid, who plays Alice Horton, is currently separated from her husband of over thirty years, actor Philip Bourneuf. She lives alone in the lovely Los Angeles suburb of Brentwood, and her house is evidence of her green thumb and skill in interior decorating.

Bill Horton is portrayed by Edward Mallory. Besides acting, he is a talented screenwriter and songwriter and says he would eventually like to work his way into the directing end of television. Recently divorced from actress Joyce Bulifant, he lives alone in a Los Angeles suburb and retains a close relationship with his young son, Edward junior.

John Clarke, who has been in the serial from its beginnings, has done a brilliant job portraying emotionally disturbed Mickey Horton for the past year and a half. John entered show business as a member of a folk-singing trio and was attending law school when he won his lawyer role on this serial. John is happily married to his wife of seventeen years, Patti. They and their three children—Josh, eleven; Heidi, nine; and Mindy, eight—live in Los Angeles and take advantage of their year-round sunshine by boating, snorkeling, and going on family outings.

The demanding role of Dr. Laura Horton is played by Rosemary Forsyth. Before joining this serial, she appeared in numerous films and played opposite such leading actors as Dean Martin, Jackie Gleason, Glenn Ford, and Cliff Robertson. It's not hard to

64   THE SERIALS

believe that before deciding on an acting career, Rosemary was a top fashion model. Today she is divorced and lives in a Los Angeles home with her ten-year-old daughter, Alexandra.

Bachelorette Suzanne Rogers likes to kick up her heels, something her character of Maggie Horton couldn't do for a long time because she was supposed to be crippled. Suzanne started her career as a Radio City Music Hall Rockette in New York City. A native of Colonial Heights, Virginia, Suzanne has an independent and strong personality. She says she wasn't very pretty in high school, which is hard to believe of someone who is often described as a young Susan Hayward. Suzanne came to Hollywood with the road tour of *Funny Girl*. From there on, success came naturally.

Margaret Mason, who plays Linda Phillips, is happily married to producer-writer Nick Alexander. Margaret, her husband, and her stepdaughter, Lisa, live in the San Fernando Valley. But life wasn't always rosy for Maggie. In 1968 she underwent surgery for cancer, had a heart attack and needed open-heart surgery, and had double pneumonia. Through her strong belief in God, plus the support of her family, she recovered and was back to work within two years. Before her illnesses, Maggie says she would fret over everything and anything. Now she calmly faces any problem. Maggie comes from Valley Forge, Pennsylvania, and enjoys swimming, horseback riding, and golf.

If you think Julie and Doug Williams play convincing love scenes, they get a lot of practice! Perhaps the most celebrated daytime romantic duo, actors Bill Hayes and Susan Seaforth Hayes made the cover of *Time* magazine last year as the "king and queen

Left:
Linda Phillips (Margaret Mason) has never lost her love for Mickey Horton (John Clarke).

Right:
An operation and therapy enabled lovely Maggie Horton (Suzanne Rogers) to walk again.

Days of Our Lives 65

of daytime TV." They met on this serial; following a four-year courtship, they married on October 12, 1974, in Bill's North Hollywood home, where they reside today. This is Susan's first marriage, while Bill has three daughters and two sons from a previous marriage. He recently recorded his second album, "From Me to You, With Love." Both Hayeses are active church members in their North Hollywood community. When their hectic schedules permit time away from the show, they hit the road for cross-country appearances and charitable events.

Lawyer Don Craig may be a loser at love on the serial, but in real life actor Jed Allan could not be happier. He and his wife of nineteen years, Toby, live in a spacious house in Tarzana, California, with their three handsome sons: Mitch, sixteen; Dean, fourteen; and Rick, eleven. Jed is very proud of his wife the businesswoman. Toby is co-founder of the thriving Los Angeles-based firm Renta Yenta. Jed's rugged good looks are seen in various TV commercials, and he is host of the syndicated series "Celebrity Bowling."

Since beginning her role of Dr. Marlena Evans, Deidre Hall has remarked that her friends feel the character is more like herself than her previous role on "The Young and the Restless." Like Marlena, Deidre is independent and strong and recently separated from her husband, singer-composer Keith Barbour. Deidre's twin sister, Andrea, lives in Florida but has tried her hand at acting. Andrea played Deidre's bad twin on Deidre's Saturday morning kiddie show "Electro Woman and Dynagirl." One who likes to do things herself, Deidre has been fixing up a cottage in Hollywood.

Amanda Howard is portrayed by lovely Mary Frann. Mary entered the acting field after becoming America's Junior Miss in 1961. Following a brief stint as the weather girl for her hometown St. Louis station KSD-TV, she moved to Hollywood. Mary and her husband, talent agent T.J. Escott, recently moved into a dream house high atop the Hollywood hills, which they share with T.J.'s son, Christopher. How does Mary keep her great shape? "She never eats!" laughs good friend and co-star Susan Seaforth Hayes. Mary, Susan, and the other women on the show have organized an exercise class that gets together during lunch breaks.

Two unsuccessful attempts at matrimony have not soured Joe Gallison on the institution. He says he's definitely in the market for number three! When not playing his Dr. Neil Curtis role, Joe is a passionate golfer and enjoys swimming and refinishing furniture in his Los Angeles home.

Peter Brown, who plays Greg Peters, is another male star of this show who has not had much luck in marriage. Three past failures have made him a bit cautious, although actress-model Jean Carlson shares his life at the moment. A rugged outdoorsman, Pe-

A barbershop quartet? No, just castmates Edward Mallory, Robert Clary, John Clarke, and Jed Allan having a good time at a "Days" party.

Lovely Deidre Hall is much more like her current character, Dr. Marlena Evans, than the one she played on "The Young and the Restless."

Gentle and kind to all living things is the way of both Mary Frann and her character, Amanda Howard Peters.

Days of Our Lives 67

Each of these people has problems: Dr. Greg Peters (Peter Brown, on the left), Rebecca LeClair (Brooke Bundy), and Eric Peters (Stanley Kamel).

Tragedy and unhappiness seem to follow Phyllis Curtis, but Corrine Conley has found nothing but joy with her husband, Bonar Stuart.

ter adores swimming, tennis, and motorcycling in northern California. The light of his life is his eleven-year-old son, Matthew, with whom he shares an exceptionally close father-son relationship. Prior to joining the show, Peter starred in two nighttime TV series, "Lawman" and "Laredo."

Phyllis Curtis may be unlucky in love, but Corine Conley has a happy life with her husband, Bonar Stuart. She is also the mother of two sons, Curtis and Tony. Corinne was born in New Jersey, and knew by the time she was in fourth grade that she wanted to be an actress. She made her stage debut in second grade as an assistant witch in the school production of *Hansel and Gretel*. Although her character is completely dependent on a man, Corinne has a true sense of self. She enjoys collecting antiques but has to have a house sale every now and then because she and her husband collect too many antiques to fit into their home.

10 Another World

Since its May 4, 1964, debut on NBC, "Another World" has frequently topped the Nielsen ratings for daytime viewing and is popular with an audience as diverse as the population of the country. The serial has set two precedents in its relatively brief run: a spinoff of "Another World" entitled "Another World, Somerset" began March 30, 1970; and "Another World" became the first hour-long daytime serial on January 7, 1975.

Although it was the first daytime drama to deal with the controversial subject of abortion, over the years "Another World" has focused mainly on the characters, dramatizing the good and evil in people.

The action takes place in the midwestern town of Bay City. When the show initially went on the air, Jim and Mary Matthews were attempting to deal with the growing pains of their three children, Pat, Alice, and Russ.

Jim and Mary were happily married for more than twenty-five years, and their dispositions complemented one another. While Jim was easygoing, patient, and able to maintain perspective even in the most dire emergencies, Mary was high-strung and quick to display emotion. They were equally supporting and loving as parents, but Mary was satisfied to make rearing children her full-time career. They maintained a mutual respect, but Jim had the final say. Daughters Pat and Alice inherit this trait of female subservience, which causes them much grief in their later lives. While finances were never a burden for the Matthews family, Jim and Mary tried to teach their children that happiness could not be bought and sold; it came from within.

Jim, Pat, Alice, and Russ Matthews suffered a tremendous loss when Mary fell victim to sudden heart failure and died. All grieved, but the recollection of their many wonderful times together enabled them to cope.

Willis's unpredictable nature has mellowed since Leon Russom took over the role.

Of all the Matthews children, blonde, fair Alice had the most severe problems trying to deal with her upper-class status. Always soft-spoken, highly emotional, and extremely sensitive, she often questioned the justice of inherited wealth. She was hesitant to become involved in a romantic relationship, but once she committed herself, it was a total, all-encompassing involvement. Nevertheless, all her relationships with the opposite sex meant little until Steven Frame entered her life.

Born on the wrong side of the tracks, Steve was a determined, independent man who had made good. While stubborn and bull-headed in his business dealings, he mellowed when he was around Alice—and she delighted in Steve's strength of character and strong convictions. They were seemingly the perfect match, as their strengths complemented one another. Alice's parents had difficulty adjusting to Steven's brusque manner, but when they saw the joy that he brought into their daughter's life, they prepared to welcome him into the family.

The inseparable duo turned into a tragic triangle when Rachel Davis set her sights for Steven. One of daytime TV's most complex villainesses, Rachel was raised in a poor and fatherless home. But she maneuvered those two strikes against her cunningly. Ashamed of her past, Rachel valued possessions more than most people. She desperately wanted to escape from her poverty-stricken background. Rather than improve herself as a person, she tried to better her life through marriage to a wealthy husband. Her first target was Alice's younger brother, Russ, a handsome young doctor. Rachel and Russ were married.

Unhappy with her struggling young intern, Rachel made Steven Frame her next target. Not only was he attractive and wealthy, but he also was loved by the pretty and wealthy Alice. Rachel decided that Alice was due for a little heartache. Rachel also felt that she could understand Steve better than Alice ever could because they came from similar backgrounds. Rachel was convinced that, although Steve had established himself in the business world, Alice was unable to appreciate his roots and his struggles to survive.

Following a lover's spat with Alice, Steve was miserable. Taking advantage of his extremely vulnerable state, Rachel made herself very available. The one night they spent together resulted in her pregnancy, years of heartbreak for Steve and Alice, and a divorce for Rachel and Russ.

While Steve offered child support for their son, Jamie, he refused Rachel the love that she desperately craved. Her greed and her selfish motives ultimately made Rachel a very unhappy woman. A brief subsequent marriage to restaurateur Ted Clark also ended in divorce. She floated directionless until Mackenzie Cory entered

70 THE SERIALS

her life. Extremely wealthy and quite a few years older than Rachel, Mac was a kind man, generous with his emotions as well as with his money. In Rachel he saw a lonely and misunderstood individual. His love and patience broke through her uncompromising exterior and discovered a soft, vulnerable woman. Rachel grew to understand his compassionate nature. They fell in love and were married.

Just as Steve and Alice appeared to have at last found the happiness that had eluded them for so long, Steve was killed in a helicopter crash. His death brought about several changes in Alice's life. For the first time, she was forced to function without a man to dictate to her and advise her. Since she inherited controlling interest in Steve's business, she also had the company's future in her hands.

Steve's younger brother, Willis, came to Bay City. Alice befriended him, giving him a job with Frame Enterprises. Because Willis had never before known power or money, he lied and cheated in an attempt to take over the company. His underhanded motives were discovered, and he was relieved of all duties. In fact, Alice developed a shrewd business sense and today is very much her own woman.

Pat physically resembles her younger sister, Alice, but there the similarity ends. The oldest of the three Matthews children, Pat developed a sense of mischief and adventure as an adolescent. She suffered severe growing pains and constantly tried to gain more independence, severely trying her parents' patience and often threatening their sanity. But because she was their oldest child and their first test as parents of a teen-ager, they gradually loosened the reins.

Pat was in a hurry to grow up. While still in her teens, she entered into a passionate love affair with a young man named Tom Baxter. Her naïveté and lack of maturity became apparent when she became pregnant. Because he refused to marry her, Pat had an illegal abortion and almost died from resulting complications.

Pat despised herself and hated Tom. During a bitter argument, she shot and killed him.

Lawyer John Randolph agreed to defend Pat against a charge of manslaughter. A long-time widower, he was quite a few years older than his client but found himself much attracted to her. A kind and patient man, John's initial interest was more as a sympathetic father figure; he had a daughter, Lee, about Pat's age. But Pat soon filled a deep void in his life, and he fell in love. Her persistence paid off as he won not only his client's acquittal but also her heart.

Pat and John's union produced twins, Michael and Marianne. Following years of a seemingly happy marriage, Pat suffered an identity crisis. She questioned whether she and John had ever

Although John Randolph (Michael Ryan) has been in marital trouble in the past, he cannot understand why his wife wants a divorce.

Another World 71

truly shared their innermost feelings. Experiencing a deep-seated need to lead her own life and establish a separate identity, she asked John for a divorce.

Russ Matthews has never proven to be anything but a total joy to his family and friends. A soft-spoken, even-tempered man, his selfless desire to give to others has led him to a career in medicine. Russ has never been extravagant. What he wanted from life was a successful career and a happy home, similar to the environment in which he had grown up. He never planned for his career to take precedence over his personal life, but a tragic sequence of events left him no choice.

His first marriage, to Rachel Davis, proved to be a disaster. He put up with her selfish ways until he learned that he was not the natural father of their son, Jamie. He later fell deeply in love with a nurse, Cindy Clark. Wedding plans were temporarily put aside when she was stricken with a rare blood disorder. They later married in the hospital chapel, but Cindy died shortly thereafter. He is currently married to Sharlene Watts. The newlyweds were happy until Russ discovered that she had once been a prostitute. He is trying to forgive her, but knows he cannot forget.

One Bay City resident who has a heart of gold and a backbone of steel is Ada Davis McGowan. Because her husband abandoned her, she had to raise her daughter, Rachel, in a fatherless home. And since Rachel was a thoughtless troublemaker, Ada had little time for her own happiness. She was briefly happy while married to garage mechanic Ernie Downs, but he died of heart failure after they had been together only a brief time. Ada was alone again.

It seemed only just that this warm, loving woman should meet her match in widower, Detective Gil McGowan. The two filled each other's tremendous need for companionship, and married. Although they were not wealthy, they were rich in happiness and contentment. The birth of a daughter, Nancy, was a dream come true, and she is a comfort to Ada since Gil's death.

One woman who has interfered countless times in the lives of others is wealthy Iris Carrington, daughter of Mackenzie Cory. Money has always been her base of power, and she has always let it do the talking.

Iris has never experienced a tender, loving relationship because she always has ulterior motives for her actions. She compares any man who tries to get close to her to her father, whom Iris idolizes. She used every trick in the book to destroy her father's marriage to Rachel because she was unable to think of another woman's stealing her daddy's love away. Her own unsuccessful marriages, to Eliot Carrington and Robert Delaney, only further embittered her against all men—except one. She is also alienating her teen-age son, Dennis, as she smothers him with her overprotectiveness.

Once again Alice seems to have found love. Here actress Susan Harney has some fun on the set.

The backbone of the Matthews family is Jim, played by Hugh Marlowe.

The young men affected by their parents' problems are Jamie Frame (Bobby Doran, on the left) and Dennis Carrington (Mike Hammett), who are also real-life good buddies.

Iris Carrington (Beverlee McKinsey) is still suffering from losing her "daddy" to Rachel.

The stalwart of the Matthews clan, Jim, is portrayed by Hugh Marlowe. While "Another World" is his first daytime stint, he is instantly recognizable to viewing audiences, having starred in many major motion pictures during the 1950s. Hugh has his life very much in order. A self-described family man, he has two grown sons, Jeff and Chris, from his first marriage to actress K.T. Stevens. Today he is happily married to his second wife, Rosemary. They and their young son, Hugh junior, reside in a luxurious apartment in Manhattan's Upper West Side, where the actor enjoys tending his home-grown vegetables and doing woodwork.

Susan Harney faced a difficult task when she joined the cast of "Another World" in 1975. She assumed the role of Alice Frame after the actress who had portrayed her for eleven years left the show. Susan is a real country gal living in the heart of New York City! She was born and raised in Murfreesboro, Tennessee, and is extremely athletic, favoring horseback riding and ice skating. Single, Susan is totally feminine and says that she hopes one day to marry and have a large family.

Multifaceted Rachel Davis Matthews Clark Frame Cory is convincingly portrayed by talented Victoria Wyndham. Although she loves her role and thinks it is one of the best on daytime television, Viki says it has created a slight problem in her personal life.

Another World   73

Mackenzie Cory (Douglass Watson) could not get his wife to forgive him for his one night of indiscretion.

Once a troublemaker, and now in trouble, Rachel (Victoria Wyndham) is hoping for a brighter future.

"I can't vacation anywhere in the United States and get any peace. It seems that anyone who works in or visits resorts watches 'Another World.' It's difficult to get any privacy." Very much a family lady, Viki treasures those private moments spent with her husband, theatrical producer Wendell Minnick, and their two young sons, Darian and Christian. All four reside in upstate New York. Their spacious house is situated on lots of acreage, so the actress can indulge in one of her favorite pastimes, horseback riding. She's also a very talented artist. All the sculptures her character creates on the show are Viki's works of art.

When Douglass Watson joined "Another World" and brought the character of Mackenzie Cory to life, he was a highly reputed stage actor and the recipient of just about every theatrical award in existence. He entered the acting profession after World War II, during which he was a much-decorated bombardier. Today he and lovely wife, Eugenia, reside in suburban Connecticut with their three children. Douglass loves his role on "Another World" and jokingly comments about the distinct advantage to working on daytime TV: "I've been offered free fishing and sailing trips while on vacation . . . free dinners in restaurants . . ."

Actor Leon Russom portrays Willis Frame. Currently a bachelor, he has for the past few years been seeing actress Andrea Marcovicci, with whom he appeared on the now-defunct serial "Love Is a Many Splendored Thing." The majority of Leon's time is consumed by his career. He appeared in the film *The Catonville Nine* and on numerous TV commercials. He lives in the Chelsea section of Manhattan.

Beverly Penberthy has portrayed Pat Randolph for almost nine years. Her attractive face has graced many TV commercials, but since the serial expanded to an hour, she finds free time a rare commodity and commerical auditions a virtual impossibility. Michigan born and bred, she worked as a professional model prior to opting for an acting career. In May 1976, she exchanged wedding vows with businessman Don Chickering. The happy couple reside in upstate New York with Beverly's three children from a previous marriage, Mark, Leslie, and Elizabeth. The actress claims that one of her most awkward moments was at a White House reception for UN Ambassador William Scranton. When other guests discovered "Pat Randolph" was in their midst, Beverly unwittingly stole the show!

Actor Michael Ryan, who describes himself as a traditional family man, divides his working time between his John Randolph role and appearing in off-Broadway productions. He is happily married and devoted to his three sons, Michael junior, Christopher, and Anthony. Before choosing an acting career, Michael attended St. Benedict's College, where he seriously contemplated devoting his life to the priesthood. Today, all five Ryans lives in a brownstone in Greenwich Village.

Although "Another World" was David Bailey's first role on daytime TV, he was recognizable to audiences everywhere from his many TV commercials and modeling stints. He's the third actor to play Dr. Russ Matthews, and he holds the character very dear. And he didn't mind the extra work when "Another World" expanded to an hour. He claims the longer the day and the heavier the schedule, the more he likes it! Personal happiness has not eluded him either. He and his wife, Lois, are very compatible and have ventured into joint professional projects; in 1976 she produced and he starred in the off-Broadway production *Pavillion*. They hope to work together again soon. David is devoted to his nineteen-year-old daughter from his first marriage and to his and Lois' son, Xander.

Actress Laurie Heineman has taken the serial by storm with her touching portrayal of Sharlene Watts Matthews. Single, Laurie lives on Manhattan's Upper West Side in an apartment that she calls "certainly no palace!" She enjoys performing Shakespeare and made her film debut in *Save the Tiger* which starred Jack Lemmon.

Constance Ford loves her character, Ada McGowan, because "she's motivated by love, mainly her children, her home, her husband." When Connie joined the show in the mid-1960s, she brought an impressive list of screen and stage credentials with her. A former cover girl and model, she's single and lives on Manhattan's East Side. Besides acting, she loves traveling, tennis, and swimming. Unlike Ada, she hates to cook!

Before becoming an actor, Dolph Sweet was employed as a New York City cab driver and a drama professor at Barnard College. The honeymoon's still on for him and his wife of four years, Iris. The couple share a love of chess, gourmet cooking, and each other. Dolph has enjoyed his role of Gil McGowan on "Another World" and names it a distinct advantage when people recognize him. "It's nice when you go into a hotel in a strange city and you say, 'Will you cash my check?' and they say, 'Sure, we know you!'"

Of her characterization of Iris Carrington, Beverlee McKinsey says, "She's crazy, impulsive, exciting, but never boring!" Beverlee left her native Oklahoma and headed for the bright lights of Broadway after receiving a bachelor of arts degree in drama education. Although she's divorced, there are two important men in her life: her seventeen-year-old son, Scott, and her longtime beau, actor Berkley Harris.

The center of recent troubles, Sally (Cathy Greene) was adopted by Alice.

Gentle and kind is Dolph Sweet, who played the tough detective Gil McGowan.

Another World 75

11
The Doctors

As its name implies, "The Doctors" is a serial that deals primarily with the personal and professional lives of medical people. It first hit the NBC airwave on April 1, 1963.

For years, the chief of staff at Hope Memorial Hospital was Dr. Matt Powers. A calm, objective man, his common sense and reliability make him a trustworthy confidante. His wife, Dr. Maggie Powers, is also a highly intelligent, skilled physician. Dedicated to their work, Matt and Maggie had yet been able to separate their personal and professional lives, and maintained a close, loving relationship. Through years of sharing, Matt had adopted his wife's sentimental family attitudes.

Matt and Maggie's existence was violently disrupted by devious, vindictive Dr. Paul Summers. Summers had met Matt years ago when Summers' wife had a baby. Matt had delivered the child, which turned out to be severely retarded. The guilt of bearing such a defective infant so affected Summers' wife that she had to be committed to an institution, where she died. Summers blamed Matt for turning his world upside down and swore, that, regardless of how long it took, he would avenge his misfortune.

When Summers eventually returned to Hope Memorial, his bitter feelings intensified as he saw Dr. Matt Powers, the happy family man. As part of an extremely well laid scheme, Summers became romantically interested in a confused young art student and hospital volunteer, Stacy Wells. He encouraged Stacy's drug habit. While she was under the influence of a hallucinogen, Paul convinced her to pull the plug on a hopelessly ill patient, Joan Dancy. Paul had earlier overheard Matt say that he believed that terminally ill patients should be allowed to die with dignity. Paul set about framing Matt for Joan's death.

The strain of this accusation altered Matt's stable personality. Stress caused him to lose his self-confidence and determination and he resigned as chief of staff. The district attorney assumed the move to be an admission of guilt. By no small coincidence, Dr. Paul Summers was appointed temporary chief of staff of Hope Memorial Hospital. He and Stacy married.

Over the years, Matt and Maggie Powers found that they could cure most people's illnesses, but unfortunately they found no prescription for their children's anguish. Matt's son from a previous marriage, Mike, had so admired and respected his father that he chose to become a doctor and try to live up to the Powers family tradition.

Matt tried to alleviate any pressures on Mike and to stress Mike's individuality, but it was easier said than done. Mike had a tender, sympathetic nature in his professional duties, but he also had a fiery temper and little tolerance where his wife, Toni, was concerned. Although he loved Toni deeply, he was unable to leave his frustrations at work, and she suffered the brunt of his hostility.

After losing a young patient, Mike almost lost his sanity. He left Toni with only a note explaining that he had some soul-searching to do. He did not know that he had left a pregnant wife. Returning a year later, he was shocked to learn that he was the father of Michael Paul. Toni and Mike reconciled, but his stormy disposition, combined with his wife's need for love and security, made their union a constantly rocky affair.

Dr. Althea Davis's medical prowess is exceeded only by her history of broken love affairs. A fiercely independent woman,

Will newlyweds Jerry and Penny Dancy (Jonathan Hogan and Julia Duffy) always be so happy?

The Doctors

Althea is also emotionally high strung. In her personal or professional life, once she commits herself to a project, it is an all-encompassing involvement.

Althea's grown daughter from her first marriage, Penny Davis, has inherited her mother's stubborn streak. As a result, neither mother nor daughter seems to know the meaning of the word compromise. They frequently come to blows over family matters.

Althea has had an on-again, off-again love affair with her second husband, brusque, brash Dr. Nick Bellini. Their similar take-charge attitudes and overbearing presence has made them incompatible for any stretch of time. It seems that they cannot live with or without each other. Only Althea's ability to laugh at herself has enabled her to recover from her numerous heartbreaks.

Steve and Carolee Aldrich appeared to be sitting on top of the world. Both had successful careers: he as an obstetrician, and she as head of nursing at Hope Memorial. Their marriage seemed happy and both adored their children—Billy, Carolee's adopted son; Erich, Steve's son by a previous wife; and Stephanie, their own daughter.

Carolee's verve and bounce offset Steve's more conservative manner. Then Erich's mother, Dr. Karen Werner, arrived in town to wage a custody suit against the Aldriches. Tensions rose, and Steve and Carolee began to battle over meaningless things. Although Steve and Carolee were ultimately awarded custody of Erich, Steve felt that Karen should have certain parental privileges. Carolee, believing that her husband was being too accommodating toward Karen, had to face bitter arguments as part of her daily life.

Carolee received an attractive job offer in New York. Deciding that she needed time to be by herself, she seized the opportunity to interview for the job as a temporary escape. But once away, she became homesick for her family. She returned home unannounced—only to find Steve in his bathrobe, and Dr. Ann Larimer with him!

Ann is a strikingly attractive redhead with fiery green eyes, and a temperament to match. A determined woman, she would stop at nothing to get what she wanted. And she wanted Steve Aldrich. Ann and Steve had shared a teen-age romance and a brief marriage, but until Carolee's departure, they had seemed no more than good friends.

As a horrified Carolee stared at the two lovers, a number of thoughts flashed through her mind. How long had Steve and Ann been lovers? Was she the last to know about their affair? She felt deceived not only by her husband, but by friends as well. Carolee felt that she could never again love or trust anyone. She quickly turned and ran away.

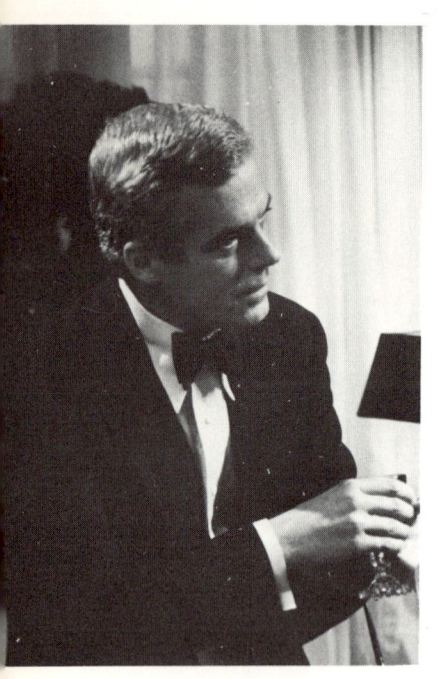

While his wife was missing, Dr. Steve Aldrich (David O'Brien) became involved with two women.

The Aldrich family: mother Mona Kroft (Meg Mundy), Jason (Glenn Corbett), and Steve (David O'Brien).

Steve later received a message from Carolee stating her disillusionment. She said they were through. Unbeknown to him, Carolee entered a mental institution after suffering a nervous breakdown. She lost all sense of time and identity. Someone knew of her whereabouts, however; it was Paul Summers, and he alerted Ann Larimer.

Always one to give good advice, Dr. Matt Powers (Jim Pritchett) now finds that he needs advice. His wife, Maggie (Lydia Bruce), is by his side.

The Doctors 79

Steve's children blamed him for Carolee's absence; they said he must stop seeing Ann or risk losing their love. Ann, fearful of losing Steve, did not tell him about Carolee's condition.

James Pritchett, much like his character Dr. Matt Powers, is a dedicated family man. His favorite times are private moments in his home on Manhattan's Upper West Side, shared with his wife, Cindy, and their three children: Laura, nineteen; Shelley, sixteen; and Kyle, ten. Jim frequently appears in off-Broadway productions.

Pritchett is a close friend of his TV wife, Lydia Bruce, who plays Dr. Maggie Powers. Because she and her husband, actor Leon B. Stevens, are nature enthusiasts, the pair usually escape on weekends from their Manhattan apartment to a country house in New Hampshire, where they enjoy horseback riding and long hikes. Both are avid theatergoers as well as Broadway stars.

When offered the role of Dr. Paul Summers, Paul Carr had to move from Los Angeles to New York. He now sublets an apartment in the city's Greenwich Village section. Paul is divorced, with no intentions of remarrying. He misses his two teen-aged daughters, Christina and Alexandria, with whom he maintains an

The tragic figure of Stacy Wells Summers, as played by lovely Leslie Ray.

80 THE SERIALS

extremely close relationship. He loves good food and eating out in restaurants, but at home he makes a terrific *linguine* clam sauce!

Actress Leslie Ray had to leave her starring role in the Broadway hit *Godspell* because her role of Stacy Wells Summers became too time-consuming. Slender, petite, and dynamic, she's devoted to her career as an actress, singer, and dancer. One day, though, she definitely wants to marry.

Armand Assante, who portrayed Mike Powers, describes himself as basically a loner. A passionate theatergoer, he enjoys shows whether he is starring in them or a member of the audience. He also likes good books, poetry, and ballet. He is a bachelor, and resides on Manhattan's Upper West Side in an apartment overlooking the Hudson River.

Elizabeth Hubbard, who has played Dr. Althea Davis since the show started, considers her most important role in life being mother to her seven-year-old Jeremy. She has appeared on Broadway and in 1976 was named Best Actress in a daytime special program, for her portrayal as Edith Wilson in "First Ladies' Diaries: Edith Wilson." In whatever spare time she can muster, Liz enjoys gardening, snow skiing, singing, and playing the piano.

Penny Davis is played by Julia Duffy. Moving to New York from her native Minneapolis was a difficult transition for Julia because she is close to her family. But her companion for the last few years, actor Jerry Lacy, seems to have made the situation more bearable. They met while both appeared on the serial "Love of Life," in which Jerry still plays Rick Latimer. Julia is frequently seen on TV commercials.

Carolee Simpson Aldrich is portrayed by Jada Rowland, who will be familiar to serial fans from her ten-year stint on "The Secret Storm," where she played Amy Kincaid. Jada lives in Manhattan with her young son, and for relaxation, she enjoys oil painting. Jada is a close friend of her former "Secret Storm" co-star, actor David O'Brien.

David O'Brien is a man who cherishes his privacy, but his Dr. Steve Aldrich role has made him instantly recognizable to fans worldwide. Of Irish-Scottish-German descent, he perfected his craft at London's Royal Academy. David maintains a Manhattan apartment, but he spends every available moment in his townhouse in Boston, his favorite city. A talented designer-artist, he has had several private showings in New York. He is single, and looking for Miss Right.

Geraldine Court has tried several phases of her craft. Her fine acting ability is evident in her portrayal of Dr. Ann Larimer. But she has also directed repertory and off-Broadway productions. Single and enjoying it, she lives in Greenwich Village in an apartment adorned with antiques and lush greenery.

12
General Hospital

"General Hospital" is ABC's longest-running soap, having premiered on April 1, 1963. As its title says, it is about the lives of the doctors and nurses at General Hospital in Port Charles, New York. This serial, one of the first to expand to forty-five minutes, is rumored to be about to go to an hour-long format.

When hospital chief of staff Steve married Audrey, it was a disaster. Audrey, a demanding woman, was unwilling to give. The marriage ended in divorce. But as the years passed, Audrey, who had acquired a nursing degree, mellowed. A feeling remained between her and Steve but stayed just below the surface of their working relationship, although Steve knew he had never lost his love for Audrey.

When Audrey's marriage to Dr. Jim Hobart broke up, it left her with deep emotional scars. Jim felt that Audrey stripped a man of his masculinity and told her so. Doubting her femininity and desirability, Audrey took a long time to regain her self-assurance.

Once again, Steve hoped for a future with Audrey. He proposed a remarriage. His offer to adopt Audrey's young son by her second marriage, Tommy Baldwin, bound them even closer.

Neither Steve nor Audrey knew that Tommy's father, Tom Baldwin, was alive and in a Mexican jail. But one person did know this, Florence Andrews Jenkins, and she had helped Baldwin kidnap his son once before. When Mrs. Jenkins informed Baldwin that Audrey planned to remarry Steve, he had only good wishes for the union. But when he learned that Steve planned to adopt Tommy, he became angry. He felt that no man could take away his son or his son's name.

Steve and Audrey, believing their future to be bright, married and left on their honeymoon. But their return was to bring them nothing but trouble.

Diana Taylor was young and naive when she arrived in Port Charles. Looking for love, she thought she had found it in Phil

The ups and downs of the Taylor household have been exciting. Craig Huebing plays Dr. Peter Taylor, and Valerie Starrett is Diana Taylor.

Brewer. But Phil returned to his wife, Jessie. Diana was left in a predicament, for she was pregnant. Psychiatrist Peter Taylor offered to marry her and raise her child. Together they found love and happiness.

When Diana became pregnant again, Jessie urged her to tell Peter the truth, that the child, too, was fathered by Phil Brewer on the night he had raped her. Diana could not face the truth. She passed the child off as Peter's. When Peter, suspicious of such a well-formed premature child, learned the truth, he left Diana.

Phil thought that this might be his opportunity to win back Diana. He could not understand why Diana refused him. When Phil was found dead in Jesse's arms, Jesse was booked for murder. Unable to see her friend Jesse sacrifice herself, Diana confessed to the murder. In reality, neither woman was guilty; each thought the other had committed the crime.

With Jesse's encouragement, Peter and Diana reconciled and look forward to a happy future. Because Diana is unable to have any more children, she and Peter are going ahead with their plans to adopt a son.

Jeff and Monica Webber came to General Hospital as the unit's first man-and-wife resident team. They seemed to be a happily married couple dedicated to their work. But when Jeff's long-lost brother, Rick, was found alive, Monica panicked. At one time, she and Rick had been very much in love, and she had never forgotten him.

The minute Monica saw Rick, her old feelings returned. Rick tried to stay away from the couple, not wanting to destroy the happiness he thought Monica and Jeff had found. But Monica

General Hospital

The marriage of Jeff Webber (Richard Dean Anderson) and Monica (Patsy Rahn) has deteriorated now that Monica wants to go back to Rick.

wanted Rick. She concocted a plan to appear as a misused and abused wife. She pictured herself to Rick as the victim of Jeff's instability. Rick fell for it, hook, line, and sinker.

Jeff could not understand his wife's turnabout. Disillusioned, he began to take drugs. His work began to suffer, and he was almost suspended from the hospital. Steve Hardy, the Webbers' long-time friend, gave Jeff a sympathetic ear and a second chance.

Heather Grant realized that Jeff's personal life had gone wrong and decided that he might be vulnerable enough to fall for her sympathy. She wanted a meal ticket to take her out of her life of poverty. Playing on Jeff's sorrow, Heather involved him in an affair.

Believing she had found happiness with her husband, Cameron Faulkner, Leslie enjoyed being able to live a life of luxury and still practice medicine. But Cam was a jealous man where women were concerned, and he didn't like anything that took their attention away from him. Unable to conquer his jealousy, Cam systematically began tearing away every shred of happiness Leslie had.

Unable to take Cam's cruelty any longer, Leslie considered backing out of her marriage. Cam retaliated by forcing himself on her and then took Leslie off to their country cabin. In the automobile accident that followed, Cam was killed.

All Leslie wanted was to be left alone. Cam's business investments had been failing rapidly and Leslie was virtually penniless. Then another complication set in: Leslie discovered that she was pregnant. She considered an abortion, since she was afraid that the child she was carrying might turn out like Cam, but she could not go through with it. She put herself in the hands of Dr. Adam Streeter—and more than a doctor/patient relationship is developing between them.

How can a man announce to his wife that he wants a divorce, especially when she has just been released from a sanitarium and is hoping for a future with him? That is the problem facing Mark Dante.

When Mark was offered the position of chief of neurosurgery, he accepted eagerly. The only drawback was that he and his wife, Mary Ellen, would have to move from Boston to Port Charles.

Mark got into the habit of telling his troubles to the sympathetic Terri Arnett. Terri, unlucky in love, found herself attracted to Mark. As their relationship developed, Terri declared that she would not let this chance at happiness get away from her. Mark felt the same way. The barrier that stands in their way seems insurmountable.

Mary Ellen may want her husband back, but her reasons are not all that pure. She still blames Mark for the loss of their baby.

84 THE SERIALS

And she must overcome that selfish, spoiled nature that is the product of an overindulgent father.

When Rachel Ames became pregnant with her own daughter, Christine, the writers of the show took advantage of her condition, and her character, Audrey, gave birth to son Tommy Baldwin on "General Hospital." Baby Christine even played Tommy for a while, but when she began to understand what was going on around her, Rachel decided it was time Christine retired, before an identity crisis set in. Rachel lives with her husband, actor Barry Cahill, in the Hollywood hills.

The one thing John Beradino wanted most in this world was a son, and John's wife, Marjorie, blessed him with one two years ago. John also has three daughters, two by his first wife. A former baseball player for the Cincinnati Reds, John hopes his son will also excel in athletics. John is exceptionally proud of his work as Dr. Steve Hardy and has been one of the soap's staunchest defenders. He is also interested in writing and is working on a film script.

Versatile Don Chastain resurrected the character of Tom Baldwin last November. From Oklahoma City, Don almost quit acting twice. A fine musician, he starred on Broadway in *No Strings* and *Superman* and toured with Katharine Hepburn in *Coco*. The television husband of Debbie Reynolds on her now-defunct show,

Left:
It took a long time, but John Beradino finally got the son he wanted, John Anthony, when his wife, Marjorie, had their second child. Daughter Katherine Ann is also special to him.

Right:
Rachel Ames, who plays Audrey, has a good family life with her husband, actor Barry Cahill, and her daughter, Christina.

General Hospital   85

Don was a semi-regular on "Rhoda," playing the owner of the singles' bar. Divorced and the father of a son, Colin, Don appeared for a brief time on "As the World Turns." Perhaps he will add a new dimension to the character of Tom Baldwin—singing!

The sympathetic Diana Taylor is played by versatile Valerie Starrett. Although Diana has a hard time finding love, Valerie has found happiness with her second husband, businessman Barrie Gable. Valerie is the mother of a teen-aged daughter and the part-time stepmother of Barrie's children by his first wife. Valerie and Barrie have been refurbishing their beautiful California home themselves.

Craig Huebing could be considred a desirable catch by any woman. But Craig considers himself a confirmed bachelor, unlike his character, Peter Taylor. Once married to the late actress Joan Anderson, Craig now spends a good deal of his time on his boat, *The Pelican,* sailing with his friend, actor Tim O'Connor. Camping, mining, backpacking, and fishing also interest this rugged outdoorsman. And Craig has just published his first book of poems, *Daylight Moon,* which he had been working on since school days.

Emily McLaughlin's life has not been much easier than that of Jesse Brewer, but like Jesse, the character she plays, Emily has an optimistic outlook on life and a feeling that everything will turn out right. Emily has a son, Robert Lansing, Jr., by her first marriage to actor Robert Lansing. Her second marriage, to actor Jeff Hunter, ended tragically when he died a few months after the ceremony.

Being the sister of a superstar can pose problems, but Georgann La Piere takes it in stride. When she joined the show, the producers asked her to darken her light brown tresses for the character of Heather Grant. This made her look even more like her sister, Cher Allman. Georgann has been acting since she was eighteen, making her debut on "Ozzie's Girls." "General Hospital" is her first daytime role. Single, Georgann has been steady dating the youngest Hudson brother, Brett, for several years, but at this writing, they had no plans to marry.

Dedication to his career is the most important thing in life for Rick Webber. And Michael Gregory, who plays Rick, takes the same attitude. New Yorker Michael became a licensed minister while he was in the army; after his discharge, however, he followed his childhood dream of being an actor. Michael is a bachelor and part of the reason might be that he is too busy in his personal life. His own security-guard business, karate, positive mind control, and energy transfer leave him little time to meet the right woman.

Personally, Jeff Webber could wish things would go a little better for him, but Richard Dean Anderson would be the first

Two people who have found happy marriages are Valerie Starrett and her character, Diana Taylor, but both had to fight for them.

Recently recovered from an illness and looking smashing is Emily McLaughlin, who has returned to her role of Jesse Brewer.

86   THE SERIALS

to say everything is A-okay in his life. He's working on his first soap and loving it. Richard, tall and with sandy blonde hair and sensitive eyes, loves motorcycling, scuba diving, and playing the guitar and the piano. Richard played ice hockey in school, but after breaking both arms, gave it up. He still likes sports, as they keep his lean body trim.

Patsy Rahn is nothing like her conniving and selfish character, Monica Webber. Patsy originally tried for a career as a dancer, studying at the American Ballet School and Joffrey Ballet School. Later, Patsy turned to writing. When she applied for a behind-the-scenes job, her employers hired her as an actress.

Early in her career Denise Alexander dyed her auburn hair blonde for various roles. She caused a sensation when she joined "General Hospital" as Leslie. She was the first actress to be "stolen" from another network soap because she was so popular. A lover of antiques, Denise once owned her own antique shop. Animals are another of her loves. Friends know she will find a good home for any animal in need of help. The steady date of director Richard Colla, Denise helped out on his film *Ollee, Ollee, Oxen Free* last summer. It was even more exciting for her since the film's star is Katharine Hepburn.

Brett Halsey first rose to prominence in Hollywood as the star of "Follow the Sun." When jobs began to become scarce, Brett moved to Italy and became a star in their famous "spaghetti Westerns." His past serials include "Love Is a Many Splendored Thing," and "Search for Tomorrow." Now "General Hospital" has employed his talents as Dr. Streeter. You might even remember him as

Left:
Will love ever come to Dr. Leslie Faulkner? It's come to her creator, Denise Alexander, in the form of steady beau Richard Colla.

Right:
A strong, honest doctor is the way to describe Mark Dante, played by Gerald Gordon.

Left:
In love with Mark, but unable to marry him, is the fate of Terri Arnett, who is played by Bobbi Jordan. Bobbi is married to B.J. Bartlett.

Right:
She wants her husband back, but Mary Ellen Dante has to fight for him. In real life, Lee Warrick is happily married.

the original Old Spice captain, always winning the girls. His first novel has just been published, *Exile in Wonderland,* about the life of American actors in Italy in the 1960s. A second novel is planned.

Daytime fans have swooned over Gerald Gordon ever since he played Nick Bellini on "The Doctors." Once again he is playing a strong, forceful man, Dr. Mark Dante. Gordon is a bachelor known for portraying a man easy to anger on the soaps. In reality, Gerald is a gentle man, but firm in his convictions. He likes his privacy and isn't an easy person to interview.

Lee Warrick, who plays Mary Ellen, is no newcomer to the daytime scene. She was introduced on "One Life to Live." Upon leaving that show, she moved to Hollywood. Married to French actor Francois Marie Renaud, she has found the easy pace of California living to her liking. She can be seen on numerous commercials and has a film to her credit. Gentle by nature, her long, thick blonde hair adds to the appeal of her character.

Opera was the first goal set by Bobbi Jordan. But then acting took over. Singing is still important to Bobbi, and the fact that her character, Terri Arnett, owns a nightclub and considers singing an integral part of her life, made the role more desirable to Terri. She is married to writer-producer B.J. Bartlett, and they have three sons. She has been in films *(Mame, I Love My Wife),* Broadway musicals *(Company, Guys and Dolls, Send Me No Flowers),* and guested on many nighttime TV shows.

88   THE SERIALS

13 The Edge of Night

When "The Edge of Night" debuted on April 2, 1956, it was telecast over the CBS television network and was intended as a takeoff on the classic Perry Mason mysteries. The title of the show was purposely selected to coincide with its broadcast time, late in the afternoon. Over the years, programming changes dictated an earlier time slot, and "The Edge of Night" began to depart from its Perry Mason origins. On December 1, 1975, the serial was sold to ABC, returned to its late afternoon airing, and it regained some of the dramatic impact it had lost.

It takes place in the town of Monticello, where one of the busiest residents is Chief of Police Bill Marceau. Patience and a hatred of injustice make him ideal for his rather thankless occupation. He and his wife, Martha, were the proud parents of a foster daughter, Phoebe.

Phoebe was an extremely strong-willed young woman. She and her long-time beau, Kevin Jamison, were deeply in love. Yet his Old World ways and deep attachment to his overly protective sponsor, Geraldine Whitney, caused constant conflict in their relationship. Phoebe tried to convince Kevin that Geraldine used her wealth and hypochondria to control his life, and she demanded that he sever the apron strings.

Following an on-again, off-again relationship, Phoebe and Kevin finally wed. But living in the Whitney mansion, and Geraldine's disapproval of Phoebe's graduate studies, did nothing to strengthen the newlyweds' bond.

Phoebe's inquisitive nature could not be contained. She decided to investigate the mysterious Dr. Clay Jordan. He poisoned her drink, placed her limp body in her car, and sent it over a cliff. Her death created an enormous void in the lives of the two men who loved her: Bill Marceau and Kevin Jamison.

Mike and Nancy Karr appear to have maintained a storybook romance in over twenty years of marriage. Even skeptics would not suspect any domestic problems in this union. The two met when Nancy worked as a reporter on her father's newspaper. Lawyer Mike had tragically lost his wife, Sara, and was left to rear a baby daughter, Laurie. It was love at first sight for Nancy, who had no doubts about wanting to devote her life to her new family. She quit her job and became a full-time housewife.

Warm and gracious, Nancy proved an ideal mother and wife. Pride in her appearance and a serene inner being made her grow more beautiful with the years. Mike could not believe his good fortune in finding true love a second time. He made it a point never to take his family for granted.

Laurie grew up, married, and moved out of the family house. Nancy felt a slight twinge of sadness, but she soon happily resumed her daily chores. When the Karrs took in young Timmy Farraday for a brief time during his mother's trial, Nancy's world brightened and took on a new purpose. She and Mike fought valiantly to win legal custody of Timmy, but they ultimately lost the struggle. Nancy's depression over this loss could not be ignored. And her misery intensified when Mike began investigating an underground crime network. She feared for his safety.

Unable to shake off her worries and depression, Nancy returned to newspaper work, writing a consumer column. But it was not enough.

Nancy was also being blackmailed by the Syndicate. They wanted information on Mike's investigation, and convinced Nancy that Timmy's life was in their hands. She asked Mike for a temporary separation; although she still loved him, she needed time to think things through alone.

Laurie Karr was raised in a loving family atmosphere and longed to establish a family of her own. But her first marriage, to Vic Lamonte, proved disastrous. Her second marriage, to Johnny Dallas, an ex-convict from the wrong side of the tracks, began shakily when Nancy, thinking him unworthy of her daughter, voiced opposition.

Johnny Dallas was a big talker whose bark was worse than his bite. Throughout his life, he had never gotten a break and had had to struggle hard. But finding a woman who had faith in his abilities and wanted to set up a stable home made him want to settle down. Johnny and Laurie were married. The birth of their son, Johnny, Jr., seems to have added more steadiness to their lives.

One of Monticello's most respected citizens is Mike Karr's close friend, lawyer Adam Drake. Adam is tall, reserved, and handsome, and his gentle manner has made him the target of many women's affections.

He and beautiful Nicole Travis fell deeply in love, but his aversion to matrimony almost ended their relationship. Nicole would have done almost anything for Adam, but the one thing she demanded from him was marriage. She gave Adam an ultimatum: Either they marry or they end their affair. Adam left her, but, unable to live without her, he proposed.

Their joy was extremely short-lived. While they were on a Caribbean honeymoon, the boat on which they were sailing exploded. Adam was thrown clear. Nicole's body was never recovered, and she was presumed dead. After months of unanswered prayers, Adam resigned himself to life without her.

Helping Adam return to the business of living was Monticello's new district attorney, Brandy Henderson, who possessed both beauty and brains. Their professional relationship quickly took on a highly personal dimension, as Brandy set out to become the second Mrs. Drake. Adam's fondness for marriage had not increased, but he finally proposed.

Before a wedding date could be set, Nicole was discovered very much alive in Paris, suffering from amnesia. After regaining her memory—except for those eighteen mysterious months during which she had been missing—Nicole returned to Monticello, only to find her beloved Adam engaged to another woman.

Adam suffered mixed emotions when he found himself truly in love with two women. Nicole desperately wanted him back, but only if he came back out of love, not a sense of obligation. She tried to begin divorce proceedings so that he would feel no sense of duty toward her, but he refused to go along. Brokenhearted and defeated, Brandy returned Adam's ring, and Adam and Nicole reconciled.

Brandy was not without male attention for long. Assistant district attorney Draper Scott was enormously attracted to her. Young and brash, Scott had grown up in the shadow of a powerful, demanding father and learned early on to fight for anything he wanted. And he wanted Brandy.

Brandy was amused by his bumbling courtship and sarcastically joked about their age difference. But, in truth, her heart belonged to another. She left Monticello to begin life again in New York.

His performance as Chief of Police Marceau demonstrates that Mandel Kramer has successfully made the transition from radio serials ("Gangbusters" and "The Shadow") to those on TV. He is one of the few actors to do so. He and his wife, Ruth, have two grown daughters, Susan and Kathryn. The Kramers live in upstate New York, where they enjoy sailing and collecting art.

Kevin Jamison is played by actor John Driver. Prior to his

Delightful Brandy Henderson (Dixie Carter) lost at love, as did the man who loved her, Draper Scott (Tony Craig).

The Edge of Night

The stalwart chief of police, Bill Marceau, is played by Mandel Kramer, shown here with his wife, Ruth.

John Driver's character, Kevin Jamison, has lost his wife. But John's real wife, Gayle, is just fine.

Geraldine Whitney tries to run the lives of the people around her, but actress Lois Kibbee knows better.

work in serials, John was seen in several Broadway productions, including *Over Here!* starring the Andrew Sisters. John is a talented playwright and hopes to have one of his plays on Broadway someday. He vacated the bachelor ranks May 15, 1976, when he and actress-model Gayle Pines married in Montreal, Canada. The couple live in upstate New York.

Lois Kibbee was born into a theatrical family in Wheeling, West Virginia. She proudly boasts that the Kibbee name has been associated with acting for over one hundred years! Her convincing portrayal of Geraldine Whitney is testimony to her fine acting ability, but she has also directed over fifty plays and authored many books, including *Creative Life Book*. She is divorced and lives in Manhattan where she pursues her interests in antiques and criminology.

Lovely Ann Flood has played Nancy Karr for fourteen years. She and her husband, network executive Herb Granath, have four children, Kevin, Brian, Peter, and Karen. Their time is divided between an elegant Manhattan apartment and an upstate country house. Now that the children are growing up, Ann hopes to spend more time concentrating on a stage career.

When Forrest Compton (Mike Karr) told his mother he was going to marry, she could only say, "Well, it's about time!" He and medical researcher-teacher Jeanne Semintini were married September 28, 1975, and reside on Manhattan's Upper East Side. Forrest taught Jeanne to sail and play tennis, and she is trying to teach him to ski. Another taste Forrest has acquired since Jeanne entered his life: Italian cooking!

92   THE SERIALS

Top left:
Beautiful Nancy Karr (Ann Flood) separated from her husband to keep Beau Richardson (David Gale) from blackmailing her.

Top right:
Actor Forrest Compton and his wife, Jeanne, are very happy, but Forrest's character, Mike Karr, has many problems.

Left:
Laurie Dallas (Linda Cook) wishes her folks would get back together. Linda is happily married to Patrick Mann.

Johnny Dallas (John LaGioia) wasn't always an honest man, but his life has changed since marrying into the Karr family.

Linda Cook left college after one year at Auburn University and left to follow her heart to New York. One of her first stage roles was in the Broadway hit musical, *Carousel*. Shortly after that, she won her role in this serial as Laurie Dallas. In 1976 she married stage manager Patrick Mann.

Johnny Dallas is played by John LaGioia, who has appeared in countless TV commercials and regional theater productions. John lives alone on Manhattan's Upper West Side in an apartment walled with books about his favorite time in history: the Renaissance. He took his first trip abroad in 1976 and hopes to visit Italy, the home of his ancestors, soon.

Before assuming the role of lawyer Adam Drake, Donald May starred in the nighttime television series "The Roaring Twenties" and "Colt .45." He's a family man, devoted to his wife, actress Ellen Cameron, and their sons, Christopher and Doug. Donald is intelligent and articulate and is a frequent guest on radio talk shows, where he can discuss topics ranging from politics to daytime drama.

His wife returned to him after a disappearance of two years, and Adam Drake (Donald May) couldn't be happier.

Threats against her life have made Nicole Drake (Maeve McGuire) extra cautious.

Stunning Maeve McGuire made a welcome return to her Nicole Travis Drake role in November 1975. Her eighteen-month absence was spent in Hollywood and then in New York, to star in the ill-fated series "Beacon Hill." She loves New York, "a terribly exciting city." She is single, maintains an apartment in Greenwich Village and pursues various hobbies: antique hunting, horseback riding, and traveling.

In his role as Draper Scott, Tony Craig's first professional television part, he has made a real impact on the female members of the audience. Tony's dreams of a professional athletic career went out the window after he tore knee ligaments while playing college basketball. But after winning the male lead in a school production of *Bus Stop,* he knew where his future lay. Tony, who is single, lives in New York City and firmly believes in the power of positive thinking.

14 As the World Turns

Without question, the most popular soap on the airwaves is "As the World Turns." Created by the late Irna Phillips and Ted Corday, it premiered on CBS April 2, 1956. The show was meant to involve the audience in the families depicted, rather than just to give them exciting stories. Many of the veteran actors on the serial give the credit for the family feeling among the cast to Ted Corday, who has kept a firm yet gentle hand on his show.

Family has always been the most important ingredient of "As the World Turns." Nancy and Chris Hughes head one of the show's prominent families. Lawyer Chris and Nancy often worry about their children, Don, Bob, and Penny, concerned that the young people will not find the happiness their parents have known.

Headstrong Penny Hughes found herself involved in a series of disastrous marriages. Bob Hughes also married young, and his mother worried that his budding medical career would be interrupted. Don Hughes followed in his father's footsteps as a lawyer, but he remained something of a rebel.

Although at times Nancy seems to be meddling in her children's lives, only her wish to help those she loves motivates her. Her husband, too, has always been ready to lend a hand, although he usually keeps quiet on matters until his opinion is requested.

The strength of character Bob Hughes displays is the product of his happy home life. He was married, while still in college, to Lisa Miller, and they had a son, Tom. But restless Lisa, wanting more from life, left Bob. He picked up the pieces and found his future with Sandy Wilson, whom he subsequently married.

Once again Bob's life was disrupted. Sandy decided that she wanted to have an exciting career as a model and went to New York. In time Sandy and Bob quietly divorced.

Bob later married Jennifer, but he had to contend with her son from a previous marriage. Jen was overprotective of the child and often sided with him against her husband in family disputes. Jen finally settled down and happily awaited the birth of their child. Bob and Jen had a daughter, and each also had a career. But Jen was killed in a freak automobile accident.

Once again Bob was on his own, and this time he had a young child to raise. Bob was not willing or ready to fall in love again, but when Joyce Colman took a job at the hospital, she decided that Bob would be a good catch. She was not discouraged by Bob's reluctance to be more than just a friend.

When Bob's brother, Don, returned to Oakdale and decided to rejoin the family law firm, Joyce turned her attention to him, although she informed Bob that she would go with him if he wanted her. When Bob declined, Joyce and Don became engaged.

In truth, Bob was really interested in Valerie Conway, the woman who was to become engaged to Dan Stewart.

When Lisa Hughes married Bob, she was a golddigger. She wanted the best that life could offer, and was adventurous enough to seek it. But she has matured and become a good mother and loving daughter.

After several marriages, Lisa was a widow with substantial money. But she still longed for a husband with whom she could share her life. When Lisa met Grant Colman, she was wary; all she knew about him was what her son, Tom, told her. But Grant and Lisa fell in love.

The first obstacle they had to overcome was the fact that Grant was married. His wife, Joyce, did not want a divorce. She wanted Grant even though she had been unhappy throughout their marriage and had even had a son by him that he knew nothing about.

But Grant and Lisa were finally free to wed. Once they were man and wife, however, Lisa began to wonder if her life with Grant could be happy. Grant seemed to care only about his work, while Lisa tried in vain to build a social life for them. When Grant's jealousy became unreasonable, Lisa felt as if she were being suffocated.

A man desired by three beautiful women describes Dan Stewart. But all is not well. Dan is deeply in love with Kim Dixon and had hoped for a life with her once she could free herself from her husband, John. Keeping them apart for a long while was Dan's first wife, Susan, who hoped to remarry Dan.

When Kim and Dan first seemed to be getting together, a tornado and Kim's loss of memory separated them. When Kim regained her memory and telephoned Dan, Susan stole the taped message that Kim had left for him.

Feeling rejected, and having no hope of winning Kim, Dan sought his fortunes elsewhere. Fate brought Valerie Conway to

Oakdale, where she met Dan while she was a patient in the hospital after a plane crash.

Bob Hughes and Dan were both interested in Valerie, and she liked both men, different though they were. But it was really Dan whom she loved.

Valerie had been Kim's sister-in-law. When Valerie discovered that Kim and Dan had been lovers, she told Kim that she wanted Dan for herself. It did appear that Dan and Kim were through.

In order to prevent Valerie's marriage to Dan, Susan was persuaded to tell Kim the truth about her message to Dan. Kim's child by John had been born, and once Kim knew that Dan had never received the message, she saw a faint glimmer of hope. Kim and Dan are back together but complete happiness is not theirs.

Kim's baby has been kidnapped. And an embittered and changed Valérie fills Dan with feelings of guilt.

When David and Ellen Stewart met, he was married to someone else. After his wife found out that Ellen was the mother of their adopted son, she insisted that they move out of town. Not until his wife died did David return to Oakdale and see Ellen again. Ellen first wanted to marry David only to be close to the son she had given up at birth, but in time their marriage was one of love.

Ellen has always been strict in her ideas about raising children. She finds it hard to understand modern times, even though David gently tries to persuade her to listen to all sides of every issue. With David's firm, but gentle, hand Ellen has been able to undertake the task of being a good mother without making too many mistakes.

Often the lessons of youth are learned only through pain. Carol Hughes Stallings has had her share of pain; she often wonders if she will be able to endure the unhappiness that seems to plague her.

After Carol met and married Tom Hughes, she felt he would make a good husband. But when Tom, a promising, young lawyer, finally got his first case, he devoted so much time to his client, Natalie Banning, that Carol began to be suspicious and demanded more of his attention. Tom was not able to take the possessiveness of his marriage, and he and Carol divorced.

Carol discovered that her friendship with Jay Stallings was beginning to grow into love. She was not the kind of person to have an affair, and Jay wanted to marry her. They went to New York one weekend and returned as man and wife.

Tom, in his loneliness, turned to Natalie Banning. Natalie wanted the best that life could offer, and Tom was her ticket to it. Hiding her past, she entered into marriage with Tom, hoping to find happiness.

Helen Wagner has always been the mother figure on this show, in her role as Nancy Hughes.

Dr. Bob Hughes has lost at love several times, but Don Hastings, who plays Bob, is happily married.

As the World Turns 97

John Colenback returned to his role of Dr. Dan Stewart after pursuing a successful career on the stage and in Hollywood.

Don Hughes (Martin West) returned to his family after several years in California.

Then Jay and Natalie met, and they found they were passionately attracted to each other. They had a brief affair. Tom found out about it and separated from Natalie. Natalie wasn't about to give Tom up that easily. Needing money, she forced Jay into getting her a well-paying job before she would agree to a divorce from Tom.

Jay tried not to see Natalie, but try as he might, he could not stay away from her. Thinking that she was acting in Carol's best interests, Lisa told Carol of Jay's affair with Natalie and thus the reason for Tom's ruined marriage. Carol, distraught, ordered Jay out of the house.

Everything is topsy-turvy for this foursome. Jay loves Carol, but Carol cannot forgive him. Natalie has told Tom that their marriage did not work because of his meddling relatives and because he is still in love with Carol.

Both Don MacLaughlin and Helen Wagner, who play Chris and Nancy Hughes, have been with the serial since it premiered. They have helped form the backbone of the show and consider themselves everybody's mother and father.

Don, a widower, has little time for his hobby of photography these days. He has two sons, a daughter, and two grandchildren. Don's serial career began in radio, but "As the World Turns" became his home.

Helen Wagner likes to relax by doing needlepoint. And even if she won't admit it, she is a great cook. She is married to a producer, Robert Willey, and she once sang with the St. Louis Municipal Opera company. Although she has no children of her own, this warm and loving woman has practically adopted the entire cast of her show.

Don Hastings has done more than act his part of Bob Hughes; he has written it. His pen name is J.J. Matthew, after his three children, Jennifer, Julie, and Matthew. He and his wife, Nan, live a quiet life in upstate New York. Don hopes to have a farm someday, and envies his son because Matthew can spend so much time in the country while Don has to work in New York City.

Conniving Joyce Colman is portrayed by lovely and sensitive Barbara Rodell. Barbara is divorced and raising her son, Jonathan, in Manhattan. No newcomer to the serial world, Barbara is best remembered for her parts on "The Secret Storm" and "The Guiding Light." For a while, jobs were scarce for Barbara, and she considered retiring. But when "As the World Turns" came along, she found a new home.

New York is now home to Martin West, but he has lived in California most of his life. He is best remembered as Phil Brewer on "General Hospital." When this character was killed off, Martin considered concentrating on films. But "As the World Turns" made

98   THE SERIALS

an offer he couldn't refuse, and Martin accepted the Don Hughes role. Martin and his bride, Carolyn, have been having fun decorating their Manhattan apartment and making new friends. Both are interested in extrasensory perception. They share their home with Martin's dog, Hey, and Carolyn's cat, Morris.

The one thing Eileen Fulton (Lisa Colman) doesn't have to worry about in her private life is that her husband, Danny Fortunato, is jealous. Danny encourages Eileen in her career and produces her records. They met when they did a record together. Eileen is the daughter of a minister, and when she and Danny were married, her minister father officiated at the ceremony, held on a mountain in her hometown of Asheville, North Carolina. Although Eileen doesn't have a chance to display her vocal talents on the show, her audience is well aware of them; her personal appearances are always sellouts.

Like his character of Grant, James Douglas is a strong man. James is warm and loving, and feels that religion is very important to him, as is his marriage and family. He married his childhood sweetheart, Dawn Busby, and they have three children, Kimberly, Taryn, and Cort. Jim spends his free time writing and taking care of his property. He has always avoided publicity concerning his private life, as far back as when he was starring in the nighttime show "Peyton Place."

Gentle and serene Kathryn Hays (Kim Dixon) has found strength in her religion. She is divorced and lives with her daugher Sherri, in Manhattan. Kathryn began her career as a New York model, then moved to Hollywood, where she starred in many films and nighttime television shows.

John Colenback is returning to the role of Dan, which he originated, and is glad to be back. He feels that the people on the show are close friends, and it was like a homecoming when he returned. John, a bachelor, is also interested in producing shows. A native of Toledo, Ohio, he is a graduate of Dartmouth and made his Broadway debut in *A Man for All Seasons*.

Sexy and slinky Valerie Conway is played by fun-loving Judith McConnell. Since moving east from California, Judith has been keeping up her romance with fiancé Bob Trimble long distance, but she hopes they can be together soon. Some of her favorite things are ice-cream cones, roller coasters, and the ocean.

Bitchy Susan Stewart is always thinking of herself. But the two people Marie Masters cares about most are her twins, Jesse and Jenny. Jenny even plays her daughter, Emmy, on the show. Aristically inclined, Marie helped decorate her children's room with her own paintings. Marie is divorced from attorney Jay Harris and has been dating her former co-star, John Reilly.

The marriage of Lisa and Grant Colman (Eileen Fulton and James Douglas) was a lovely affair.

Beautiful Kim Dixon (Kathryn Hays) is finally finding happiness with the man she loves, Dan.

A woman who wants whatever she can get is Joyce Colman (Barbara Rodell).

Left:
Although Valerie Conway lost Dan to Kim, actress Judith McConnell has her own love in fiancé Bob Trimble.

Right:
There have been times when Ellen Stewart has been too strict with her children, but Pat Bruder and her husband, Charles Debrovner, are very gentle.

Unlike her character of Ellen, Pat Bruder has a wonderful relationship with her two daughters, Joy and Dawn. Married to distinguished gynecologist Charles Debrovner, Pat believes in physical exercise for her whole family.

Henderson Forsythe (David Stewart) may not be a doctor in real life, but like many doctors he enjoys playing golf. He can often be found on the links with co-star Don Hastings on their days off. At one time Henderson thought of becoming a professional athlete, but the acting bug bit him. He and his wife, Dorothea, have two sons and live in New Jersey.

Patience is a virtue; both Dr. David Stewart and Henderson Forsythe, who plays him, display the trait.

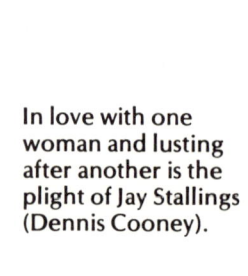

In love with one woman and lusting after another is the plight of Jay Stallings (Dennis Cooney).

100 THE SERIALS

An actor since he was a child, Dennis Cooney does not have the problems of his character, Jay. He's a bachelor and intends to stay that way, at least for the present. Growing up in live television gave Dennis the stamina for the rigors of daytime drama, but he misses the excitement of the live shows. Dennis has a great interest in antiques and has owned an antiques shop. He also leans toward directing and producing, and has done both.

It's all in the eyes, in Judith Chapman's case. Her startling blue eyes can express more than the spoken word and are an important asset to her character of Natalie. A vibrant personality, Judith loves having a good time. She made her movie debut as the star of *False Face* last year, playing both a good side and bad. She is interested in astrology and intends to keep her single status for a while.

Although he hasn't fathered any children in his role as Tom Hughes, C. David Colson has a son and a daughter in real life. He and his wife live in upstate New York, where David likes to retreat when he is not working. When asked what the C. stands for, David hedges, saying that it doesn't mean anything. He has a wry sense of humor, which infuses his "cynical side."

Whatever happens to her in life, Rita McLaughlin Walter knows that it cannot be as bad as the things that happen to her character, Carol. And Rita has great faith in God. She is married to a Baptist minister, the Reverend Norman Walter. Questioned by certain church people about how she could possibly play on a soap, Rita responds that you can learn from them. Anyone, no matter how good he thinks he is, can stray from God's path.

She wants money, and Natalie Hughes (Judith Chapman) is determined to get it.

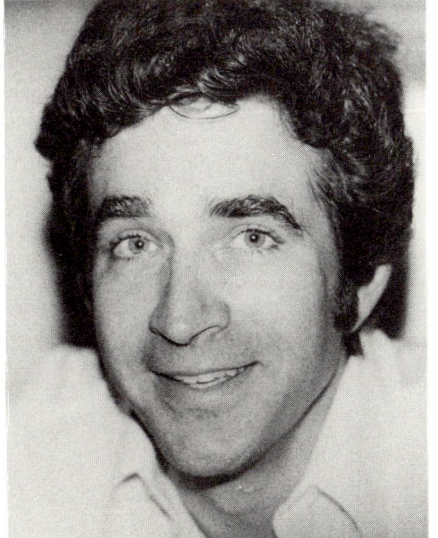

Recently married Rita McLaughlin Walter plays Carol Stallings, who is divorcing her husband on the show.

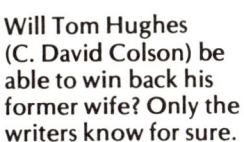

Will Tom Hughes (C. David Colson) be able to win back his former wife? Only the writers know for sure.

As the World Turns

15 Guiding Light

"Guiding Light" is the only serial to have made a successful transition from radio to television. It premiered on radio January 25, 1937, broadcast from a studio in Chicago. The story line then highlighted the Reverend Mr. Ruthledge and his friends. In time, however, the Bauer family became the focus of the serial. The third oldest daytime serial on television, "Light" made its debut on CBS television on June 30, 1952.

The central figure in the Bauer family is Bertha (Bert), who is beloved by her family and friends. A warm, giving woman, she has maintained her abiding respect for the family unit through years of struggle and heartache. Undying loyalty makes her friendship a rare, valuable commodity.

Bert endured the tragedy of an alcoholic husband, and his death in a plane crash affected her deeply. But she has always regarded her role as mother as uppermost in her life, so she has had the strength to go on. Her philosophical attitude toward life and strict adherence to the Golden Rule have proved invaluable.

Bert's two grown sons, Ed and Mike, mean the world to her. While each had a relatively happy childhood, both encountered problems upon entering adulthood. The elder, Mike, was more tolerant and even-tempered than his younger brother, and chose a career in law. An unhappy first marriage resulted in heartache but produced a daughter, Hope, whom Mike adores.

Ed is a more serious, introspective individual than Mike. As an intern, Ed worked at the hospital under the tutelage of Dr. Steve Jackson, a benevolent, erudite physician who demanded that his doctors give their full effort. He offered his vast knowledge to Ed, but the young intern was interested as well in Dr. Jackson's daughter, Leslie.

Ed and Leslie fell in love and were married, but Ed was obsessed with his career. He began to use alcohol as a release from strain. Leslie and Bert found his drinking difficult to accept because

Ed had always previously abstained from alcohol, knowing of his father's addiction.

Ed's drinking increased until it interfered with his professional and personal life. Unable to face reality, Ed left Springfield and embarked on a love affair.

During Ed's absence, Leslie and Mike fell in love. When Ed returned, Leslie planned to ask for a separation, but they spent one night together, which resulted in her pregnancy. For the sake of her child, she tried to make the marriage work, but when she discovered Ed's out-of-town affair, she called it quits. After their son, Freddie, was born, Leslie never prevented Ed from seeing the child.

Many misunderstandings and subsequent ill-fated marriages followed—Leslie to Stanley Norris and Mike to Charlotte Waring—but Mike and Leslie eventually got together and married.

Ed began dating a former patient, Holly Norris. Moody and self-centered, Holly was prone to childish tantrums when she was unable to get her own way. She had broken up with her long-time lover, Roger Thorpe, and was anxious to find someone new. When she and Ed spent a weekend in Las Vegas, she got him drunk and rushed him into a marriage. Ed regretted the move, but decided to give the impulsive marriage a chance.

Ed's world brightened considerably when he discovered he was to be a father. He blamed Holly's depression on her preg-

Although he messed up his marriage to Leslie, Ed Bauer (Mart Hulswit) has been a good father to his son, Freddie (Gary Hannoch).

Guiding Light 103

nancy, but even after their daughter Christina's birth, Holly's extreme sensitivity persisted. Unable to handle her guilt any longer, she confessed that the child had been fathered by Roger Thorpe.

Ed immediately walked out on Holly and demanded a separation. Neither one really wanted a divorce, but deep wounds to their pride prevented either of them from asking for another chance. They were divorced.

Mike and Leslie were happy for a while. When Leslie decided to enroll at the local university, Mike argued that the additional work would interfere with their home life. But when Leslie explained that she needed interests of her own, Mike relented.

Mike became preoccupied with a new client, Ann Jeffers. Ann's estranged husband grew antagonistic toward Mike. After leaving the Bauer home in a drunken stupor, Jeffers recklessly pulled away in his car, unintentionally striking Leslie. She was rushed to the hospital, where she died.

Roger Thorpe has caused a lot of heartache to many people, but he has done the most harm to himself. Tall, dark, and handsome, he was a womanizer who became adept at breaking up other people's relationships.

Holly Norris had long loved him and offered herself to him. For a while, Roger took advantage of the situation, but his conscience eventually intervened. When Holly begged him to marry her, he realized that things had progressed beyond the point of no return.

Because his shady business transactions threatened his safety and that of the people he loved, he left town.

Roger's father, Adam, is an extremely successful businessman. A widower, he accustomed himself to a single existence until he met Holly's mother, attractive divorcee Barbara Norris. Barbara was a loving woman, but the responsibility of raising Holly and two sons, Kenneth and Andrew, combined with having to maintain her career as a syndicated columnist, proved more than amply time-consuming.

Unlike his son, Adam is a highly regarded citizen. In Barbara he saw his perfect match, someone who craved companionship as much as he did. At first, because of the heartache his son had inflicted on her daughter, she refused his proposal of marriage. But unable any longer to ignore her personal feelings, Barbara finally agreed to marry Adam.

Roger Thorpe returned to town, seemingly a changed man. Although broke and friendless, he was determined to work his way up from the bottom and earn the respect of people.

He fell in love with nurse Peggy Fletcher. At first Peggy refused his advances, but Roger, who was still a bit conniving, got around her objections.

Tragedy struck Sara Werner (Millette Alexander) when her husband died on a mission to the Far East.

104 THE SERIALS

Years earlier, having been deserted by her husband, Peggy had been left alone to raise her son, Billy. As much as Peggy loved her boy, she knew that he needed a father, and Roger acted the part. Peggy soon found herself wanting to reach out to Roger as a man, but she feared his reputation. Through persistence and charm, he won her heart and they married.

Two of Springfield's finest doctors, Sara and Joe Werner were happily married for years. While much of their lives naturally revolved around the hospital, they hoped to add a new dimension to their personal lives by having a child. Sara never considered abandoning her career but was convinced she could successfully assume the roles of wife, doctor, and mother. But after years of trying to have a child, they abandoned hope.

The Werners took extraordinary interest in a homeless young boy they met in the hospital, T.J. When he was well again, they took him to live with them. T.J. seemed to fill the void in their lives, and Sara and Joe gave the boy the love and security he had never known. Tragedy struck when Joe went to India for a medical consultation and suffered a fatal heart attack. Sara and T.J. are trying to cope with their loss.

Like Bert Bauer, actress Charita Bauer is a wonderfully warm, gracious woman, who recently celebrated her twenty-fifth year on the show. As a girl, she hoped to become a dancer, but turned instead to acting. Divorced, she lives alone in Manhattan and is very close to her married son, Michael, and his family. To relax, she enjoys needlepoint and tending her plants.

The viewing audience cannot seem to get enough of Don Stewart, who portrays Mike Bauer. He is a fine singer, and his nightclub performances play to sellout audiences. As if his two careers did not keep him busy enough, Don has numerous hobbies including boating, piloting his own plane, and tending his art gallery. In 1976 Don broke his silence and confirmed reports that he was married to nurse Sue Tremble and the father of a three-year-old daughter, Heather. The Stewarts live in an apartment on Manhattan's West Side.

While Mart Hulswit is a fine actor, his Ed Bauer role is not an all-encompassing affair. He adores his wife, Maria, and his daughters, Tina and Jennifer. He relaxes by camping, hiking, skin-diving, and shell-collecting, and pursuing other family-related activities. The Hulswits live in New York City.

Dr. Steve Jackson is played by Stefan Schnabel. Born in Berlin, Stefan has lived in the United States since 1937 and is the son of famed pianist Artur Schnabel. Stefan never tires of challenging roles and has been seen in over five hundred Broadway and regional theater productions. Stefan and his wife, Marion, are the proud parents of three children, Peter, David, and Susan. They live

The person who has been with the show longest is Charita Bauer, who plays Bertha Bauer.

Don Stewart, who plays Mike Bauer, is a splendid singer as well as an actor.

Guiding Light

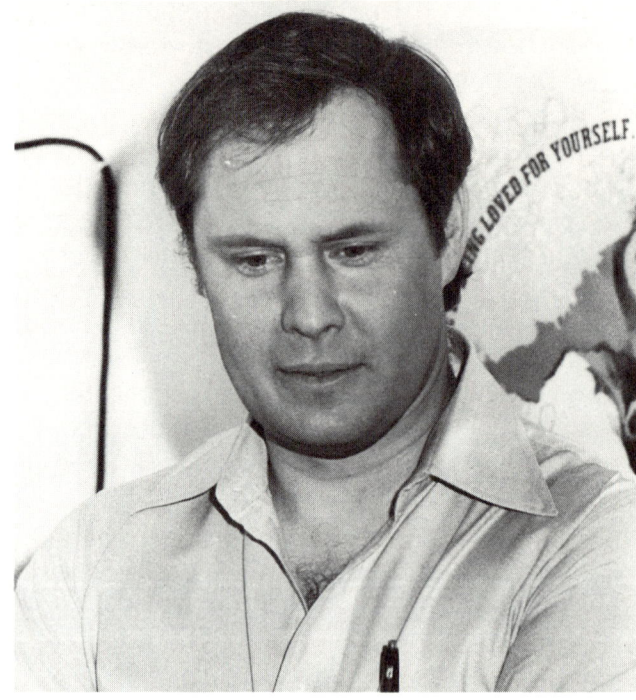

Left:
Although he lied, Roger Thorpe (Mike Zaslow) had only the best intentions—to protect his wife.

Right:
With two divorces in his past, Ed Bauer (Mart Hulswit) is looking for happiness.

in Manhattan, and Stefan bicycles to the studio every day, weather permitting.

Roger Thorpe is portrayed by Michael Zaslow. A fine stage and screen actor, he has starred in films, nighttime television, and on the Broadway stage, where he met wife Susan Hufford when both appeared in *Fiddler on the Roof*. He is proud of his wife's writing talent: Susan has had four novels published. Both love to travel, camp, and stay in touch with nature. They divide their time between a Manhattan apartment and a lovely house in Connecticut.

Adam Thorpe is played by Robert Milli. A talented actor, he is also an avid amateur photographer who has won many local contests. For the past twenty-seven years, Robert has been happily married to the former Mary Jane Mulligan. They have one daughter, Liza, and all three reside in suburban New Jersey.

Slim and bright Barbara Berjer is so full of life and energy, there's nothing she cannot do! Besides playing Barbara Thorpe, she is an excellent seamstress whose needlepoint creations frequently serve as gifts for close friends. Because her husband, Lee Foley, is a producer turned antique dealer, Barbara has acquired a love of art objects and often visits auctions and flea markets in search of bargains. Judging from their Manhattan apartment, the actress also has a green thumb, for their home is adorned with lush green foliage. Barbara and Lee have a grown son, Michael.

Serial viewers feel close to actress Fran Myers, who has practically grown up before their eyes! She has played the role of

106   THE SERIALS

Peggy since she was sixteen years old and was billed as Francie Myers. And she was an old pro even then: her acting career began at the tender age of eight, when she starred in the radio drama "The Couple Next Door." Fran's married to her former "Guiding Light" co-star Roger Newman (he played Ken Norris) and they are the parents of John Stuart. Fran and Roger hope to add another little Newman to their family in the not too distant future.

Dr. Sara Werner is played by Millette Alexander. Divorced, she's a real country gal who lives in upstate New York with her three children, Adam, Will, and Jenny. Also considered family members are their pets, which include goats, cats, a pony, some rabbits, and fish! Millette loves to garden and grows vegetables and berries on her acreage.

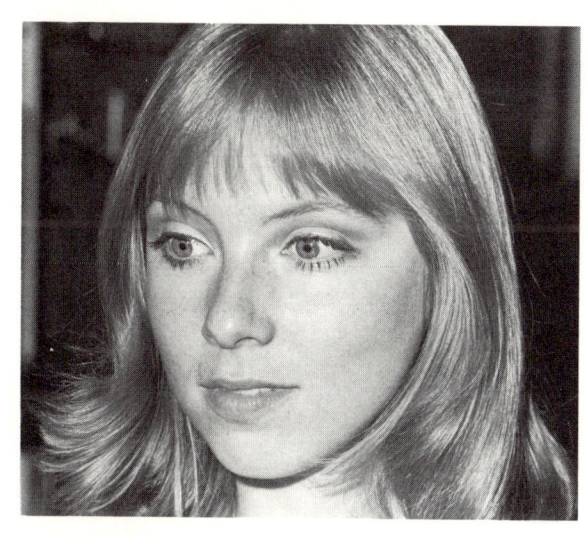

The days of innocence are behind Peggy Thorpe (Fran Myers), and she is hoping for a good future.

Guiding Light 107

16
Love of Life

"Love of Life," which premiered September 21, 1951, is the second-longest-running show on the air. It was created by Roy Winsor and sponsored by American Home Products. This CBS serial was the first to pinpoint its locale, the fictional town of Rosehill in New York.

A few years ago, it looked like "Love of Life" was going to be canceled. Then Jean Arley and Thomas de Villiers, new and talented producers, took over and changed the whole show, gradually updating both its characters and its stories.

Vanessa and Bruce Sterling had a stormy marriage the first time around. Bruce treated the compassionate Van badly by engaging in a series of love affairs. Van, not one to put up with such conduct for long, divorced Bruce.

Van fell in love again, and was planning to marry when she found out that her fiancé, Matt Corby, was actually her first husband, Paul Raven, who had been presumed dead. Paul was sent to prison for murder and later did die, in a prison riot.

Bruce became a changed man and pledged his love to his former wife. Van decided to give Bruce a second chance and is happy she did. But although Bruce has remained faithful to his wife, some of her decisions have left him skeptical. Things usually work out for the best, however.

When Caroline Aleata arrived on Van's doorstep, everyone was in for a shock. Cal was Van's niece, although Van did not know of her existence. Van accepted Cal with open arms, as did Sarah, Cal's grandmother.

Cal's life had not been an easy one. She felt alienated by her mother, Meg, and the one man she found comfort with was her stepfather, Edouard. Edouard had divorced Cal's mother, though, because of Meg's indiscretions.

With Cal in Rosehill, Meg was soon to follow. Meg met and married the town's corrupt Mayor Hart. That union was not to last long, for Hart was murdered by his son.

Meg's various marriages had left her with a great deal of money. A good businesswoman, she decided to enter into a partnership with Rick Latimer. And, of course, this led to her trapping Rick into an affair. But Meg was in love for the first time in her life.

When Cal's love life seemed to fall apart, Rick lent a sympathetic ear. In time, their friendship grew into love. Rick carefully kept his relationship with Meg a secret from Cal, not wanting to hurt Cal.

Meg was outraged when she found out that Rick and Cal planned to be married. It was inconceivable to Meg that any man would prefer her daughter over her. Thinking only of herself, Meg told Cal the sordid details of her affair with Rick. Disillusioned, Cal left for San Francisco.

Rick followed Cal, persuading her that his love for her was real. Joyously they planned a large wedding. On their wedding day, Meg took an overdose of pills and almost died, once again destroying the couple's chance for happiness.

Meg managed to keep Cal under her wing for a short time, always threatening drastic measures if Cal should marry Rick. Finally, Cal decided to call Meg's bluff and eloped with Rick to New York.

Meg is sure that she can win Rick away from Cal and is constantly finding excuses to interfere with the couple. Cal feels helpless in the situation, although she is determined not to show her jealousy. Rick is well aware of Meg's ploys and doesn't plan to be duped easily.

Cal's best friend in Rosehill is part-time reporter Betsy Crawford. When Ben Harper, Cal's half-brother, came to town, Cal tried to warn Betsy about him. Betsy refused to listen.

Ben needed to marry Betsy in order to get money from his mother. What Ben did not tell anyone was that he was already married to Arlene Lovett. Ben planned to marry Betsy, then leave town with Arlene right after the ceremony, check in hand. Meg discovered the truth and decided to withhold his money.

As Ben was planning his escape, he learned that Betsy was pregnant. Without realizing it, Ben was falling in love with Betsy. But Betsy's world came tumbling down around her. She found out that her marriage to Ben was invalid, and even though she loved him, she pressed charges against him. Ben was sent to jail.

Dr. Tom Crawford, Betsy's brother, arrived in Rosehill to help his sister and also to start his medical practice. Although Betsy protested that she no longer wanted Ben, in truth she could not forget him.

When their child was born, Ben was still in jail. Tom has encouraged Betsy to forget Ben, but now that Ben has been released from jail, he is confident that he and Betsy will get together

Completely the opposite of her sister Van, Meg (Tudi Wiggins) causes problems wherever she goes.

Love of Life

again. But Betsy is finding that life without Ben is a better life, even though she does feel compassion for him.

With her husband in jail, Arlene Lovett had to scramble to make a living. She had to support not only herself, but also her mother, who was suffering from a heart ailment. No matter what else she might be called, Arlene is a devoted daughter.

Although Carrie Lovett never approved of her daughter's involvements, she stood by her, trying to offer sound advice. When Arlene lost her job as the piano player at Rick and Meg's place, Ray Slater offered her work. Ray, an unscrupulous man who procured women for wealthy men, also had ideas of winning the sensuous Arlene for himself.

Ray introduced Arlene to wealthy Ian Russell. Ian took an immediate liking to Arlene, but he was a gentleman. He did not take advantage of Arlene; instead, he befriended her. Ray became jealous of Arlene's independence. He wanted her back in the fold, not as a steady date of Ian's.

When Arlene's mother had to have emergency surgery, Arlene was frantic. She needed money to pay the hospital bills, and Ian stepped in and paid them. Arlene tried to tell Carrie that she had saved the money, but Ray, hoping to sever Arlene's relationship with Ian, told Carrie the truth. Carrie made Arlene promise not to do anything wrong and to tell Ian that they would repay his generosity in time. Arlene did as her mother asked, but once again, Ray lost out.

When the marriage of Diana and Charles Lamont began to fall apart, Charles looked for someone to take Diana's place. Charles is basically a weak man and needs someone to support him. He thought he had found the right person in Felicia Flemming, his young grandson's teacher.

Charles and Felicia were married, and Charles had great hopes of starting life over again with a woman who loved him. But Charles was to be bitterly disappointed. Felicia was unable to consummate their marriage. Afraid of revealing their problem to their friends, Charles and Felicia pretended to be happy.

When Felicia was threatened by a would-be rapist, she accidentally shot Charles, leaving him paralyzed. Charles capitalized on the tragic situation and became demanding and overbearing with Felicia.

Felicia found a friend in Edouard Aleata. Eddie was gentle and kind with Felicia, giving her the understanding she needed. They were falling in love without realizing it.

Unable to take Charles' demands any longer, and wanting a life of her own, Felicia left their home. Trying to go after her, Charles tumbled from his wheelchair and fell into a coma.

Eddie found Felicia at the home of one of her relatives.

Felicia explained her problems to Eddie, and they made love. But Felicia did not know what happened to Charles. When she returned with Eddie, she heard the news and rushed immediately to Charles' side.

When Audrey Peters took over the role of Van, she really had not had much acting experience. She had been a dancer. Her first day on "Love of Life" started off badly when she went to the wrong studio! A sensible woman, Audrey has raised her son, Jay, alone since her divorce. Her role has become second nature to her now, and she enjoys helping and supporting the younger members of the cast.

Ron Tomme claims to be nothing like his character Bruce. He may be right. Bruce Sterling always seems to be serious, while Ron has a good sense of humor. Ron is a veteran of two years in the Army, and was married but has regained his bachelor status. He enjoys a close relationship with his co-star Audrey Peters. Ron sometimes wishes "Love of Life" was once again broadcast live.

Meg Hart doesn't laugh often, but Tudi Wiggins's deep, throaty laugh typifies the merriment in her nature. Tudi never married and has found great pleasure and success in her career. Born and raised in Canada, Tudi worked there for a good part of her life before moving to New York. She likes her character of Meg the manipulator, who is always blaming others for her problems. But Tudi is too levelheaded to be anything like her.

For many years Jerry Lacy had trouble dropping his Humphrey Bogart image, which he gained after playing Bogey in Woody Allen's *Play It Again, Sam*. A dry sense of humor is one of

Left:
Happily married and the confidants of many are Van and Bruce Sterling (Audrey Peters and Ron Tomme).

Right:
It seems that Rick Latimer (Jerry Lacy) has now found happiness, and Betsy Harper (Elizabeth Kemp) hopes he treats his new wife well.

Love of Life 111

Tom Crawford (Rick Weber) has begun to question the morals of the woman he loves.

Left:
Roxanne Gregory, who plays Cal, has two husbands: her own, Michael Harvey, and her TV husband, Jerry Lacy.

Right:
A man running from past problems is Ben Harper (Chandler Hill Harben, here shown with his real wife, Raine).

the best things about Jerry, but he can be very serious when necessary. A bachelor, Jerry has been "steady as she goes" with actress Julia Duffy for about five years. Whether or not they will marry, only they know. When not working in the city, Jerry can usually be found at his country retreat, renovating and redesigning the place.

When it was decided that Cal should be older than originally planned Roxanne Gregory was chosen to play her. Roxanne's career had centered on the stage, with side trips into a few nighttime shows and a short stint on "Somerset." She is married, and one of her luxuries is her house in the country, where she enjoys gardening.

Elizabeth Kemp defends her character of Betsy by explaining that Betsy wasn't stupid about what was going on around her, just blinded by love. Liz has had a lot of fun playing Betsy during her maturing process. Single, Liz is somewhat liberated. She does steady-date someone, but she's not saying if there is a marriage in the immediate future. Liz would like to have a chance to play comedy. Her career had centered on the stage and in commercials before the role of Betsy came along.

Rick Weber once centered his career in Hollywood, where he made numerous guest appearances on nighttime shows. His name at the time was Rick Eley. Now a resident of New York, he's enjoying his first daytime drama, as Dr. Tom Crawford. A bachelor, Rick does have a steady. He was also one of the top male models, but considers that part of his career behind him.

A serious actor, Chandler Hill Harben broke into soaps with his role of Ricco Bellini on "The Doctors." Deciding not to renew his contract, he went over to CBS to assume the vacated role of

112   THE SERIALS

Ian Russell (Michael Allison) wishes to help Arlene, but she is reluctant because he wants too much from her.

He wants Arlene, but Ray Slater (Lloyd Battista) isn't succeeding in his quest.

The third person in the triangle with Felicia and Charles is Edouard Aleata, who is played by happily married John Aniston, whose wife's name is Nancy.

Ben Harper. Chandler met his wife, Raine, when he asked if he might take her picture. They started dating, were married, and now have a son, Chandler.

Cosmopolitan John Aniston, who plays Edouard Aleata, was born on the island of Crete but now considers Eddystone, Pennsylvania, his home. He is married and has a son and daughter His good friend Telly Savalas is godfather to his daughter.

A distinguished actress, Peg Murray was pleased to take on the role of Carrie Lovett when asked. She has always enjoyed playing strong and warm women. Peg played the mother in the Broadway production of *Fiddler on the Roof*. She is interested in politics and keeps busy renovating her saltbox house.

A professional's professional is one way to describe Lloyd Battista, who brings Ray Slater to life. Lloyd has been acting since he was a child. He has a great interest in jazz, and although he has never married, he loves kids. He is a co-owner of a real estate business in Hollywood, although working in New York makes it difficult for him to spend time on it. He has performed on Broadway in *Those That Play the Clowns* and Harold Pinter's *The Homecoming*. The only thing he regrets is that he is always playing villains.

England is where tall, distinguished Michael Allinson was born and raised. But New York is his home now. Michael's good looks are just right for the suave, debonair Ian Russell. Michael and his wife, Judith, have two sons. He is an avid stage performer, hav-

Love of Life

ing taken over the Henry Higgins role in *My Fair Lady* the last two years of its first Broadway run; he also played the king in *Camelot* many times. Michael enjoys music and is an excellent duplicate bridge player.

Sensuous and a survivor is the way to describe Arlene Lovett, but if you look beneath the surface, you will find a gentle and kind human being. That part of Arlene is true also of Birgitta Tolksdorf, Arlene's creator. Birgitta was born in Germany but arrived in the United States at an early age. A top model, Birgitta broke into acting in stock. Single, she says she is in love but wants to keep it a private affair.

When Pamela Lincoln first joined "Love of Life," as Felicia, she had some opposition from her husband. He was then executive producer of the show and didn't want any gossip going around that he got her the job. Now, Pam is happier at work because her husband, Darryl Hickman, is off in Hollywood working on a new project for Norman Lear. The Hickmans have a firm and secure marriage, so they do not worry about the separation. Pam stays in New York with their two sons and is interested in producing and directing. She is also an artist and is active in projects that help people.

Helpless, weak, and almost cruel, Charles Lamont is not the nicest person to know. But Jonathan Moore, who created the part over nine years ago, has a jolly laugh and a great sense of humor. A bachelor, Jonathan was once married. When he first began on the show (it was also his first television experience) he rebelled against Charles' stuffiness. But he feels Charles has grown a lot since those days.

Arlene Lovett (Birgitta Tolksdorf) attracts many men, even when she doesn't want to.

Charles and Felicia (Jonathan Moore and Pamela Lincoln) are unhappily married.

114   THE SERIALS

17 Search for Tomorrow

On September 3, 1951, CBS-TV began broadcasting the serial that was to become the longest-running show on the air. When "Search for Tomorrow" began, its heroine was Joanne Barron. Today, younger than ever, but perhaps wiser, Jo remains the focal point of the story.

The setting of "Search" is the mythical town of Henderson, somewhere near Chicago. As the country has grown and matured, Henderson has also. The once small community is now a metropolis with modern apartment complexes and corporate businesses.

When Jo was introduced to viewers, she was the wife of Keith Barron and lived happily with him and their daughter, Patti. Tragedy struck shortly after the show's premiere when Keith was killed in an automobile accident. Jo was left to raise her daughter alone.

A kind and compassionate woman, Jo was one to stand by her loved ones, giving them support and help. When she married Arthur Tate, Jo had great hopes for happiness. But Arthur was not as strong as she had believed. Her life with Arthur was not easy, but Jo remained a faithful loving wife until a heart attack killed him.

Jo then found the strong man she wanted to marry in Sam Reynolds. But Sam still had to get a divorce from his first wife, Andrea. The divorce was long in coming because of many complications. With the divorce finally obtained, they again had to delay their marriage until Sam completed a peace mission for the UN in Africa.

Everything seemed to go wrong in Jo's life. First she had a car accident that left her blind, and then Sam was missing and presumed dead. But Dr. Tony Vincente performed an operation that gave her back her sight. The soft and gentle Jo found a match in the strong and gruff doctor.

The troubles caused by Jennifer Pace are offset by the antics of actress Morgan Fairchild.

As their love grew, Tony decided to divorce his wife. It was Jo who finally found that Marcy Vincente had faked her paralysis. Jo helped Marcy find the strength to begin life over again.

As Tony and Jo planned their marriage, Sam was found. Feeling obligated to the man to whom she had previously pledged herself, Jo left Tony. But in her heart she knew that she was making the wrong decision.

Sam was a changed man. Jealous and cruel, he could not be helped even by Jo's kindness and compassion. Prior to their wedding, Sam kidnapped Jo. Tony rescued her, and Sam was later found murdered.

Jo and Tony's marriage, for the most part, was a happy one. Tony's death from a heart attack ended it. Jo, who had always worked as the hospital librarian, left the hospital, which held so many memories for her, and embarked on a new career as co-owner of the Hartford House with her good friend, Stu Bergman.

Marge and Stu Bergman were Jo's closest friends in Henderson. Stu was an outstanding businessman, and he and Marge were the proud parents of two children, Janet and their late-in-life son, Stuart Thomas, Jr. Their marriage was a happy one, as they always looked on the brighter side of life.

Marge's death left Stu devastated. After about a year of sadness, he began to enjoy himself and even have fun as a bachelor. But Stu was looking for someone to love, never realizing that that someone was right under his nose: his secretary of many years, Ellie Harper.

Stu decided to travel. He met a widow, known to viewers only as Connie, who was out to catch him; she used every trick in the book to keep Stu and Ellie apart. Realizing that Stu had to make up his own mind, and feeling that she was no match for Connie, Ellie left town.

Without Ellie, Stu discovered just how much he missed her, but he was still flattered by Connie's attentions. It was Jo who finally brought Stu and Ellie back together, and their wedding was one of the happiest events in Henderson. They are a perfect couple; Stu is lighthearted and easygoing, and Ellie is gentle and sensible.

The life of Scott and Kathy Phillips has been a stormy one, in part because of each one's strong personality and desire for personal success. Scott and Kathy met in law school but could not marry until Scott's divorce from his first wife, Laurie, was final. Scott wanted a family of his own, but Kathy only wanted a career in law. Even though he was aware of this, Scott felt that Kathy would come around to his way of thinking in time.

When Eric, Scott and Laurie's young son, came to stay with them while Laurie was on her honeymoon, Kathy was upset but decided to adjust to the situation because it would only be temporary. But Laurie and her new husband were killed, and Scott was named Eric's guardian. Kathy was annoyed, but nothing was going to stop her from being successful. A two-career family started to take its toll on this couple, and when Kathy remained out of town on business, Scott arranged for a formal separation.

Jennifer Pace, a young client of Scott's, took advantage of the separation and maneuvered to become Scott's wife. She became pregnant, and Scott divorced Kathy and married Jennifer. But even after they had wed, Scott still longed for Kathy.

As the result of an accident, Jennifer had a miscarriage. Scott felt more and more that his life with Jennifer was a mistake. He began drinking and soon destroyed his successful law practice. Scott managed to divorce Jennifer, and Kathy helped him to rebuild his career.

Janet Bergman Walton had everything she wanted, until her husband's untimely death. Janet had acquired her parents' lively sense of humor. And her gentle nature was enhanced by a strong character. She knew she had to build a strong home life for her three children, Liza, Gary, and infant Danny. When she met and married psychologist Wade Collins, her family's future seemed secure, and she had a man she could love forever. He and Janet tried to help and aid Janet's children. Wade was the son of one of Henderson's most prominent families. After his father's death, Wade had to split his responsibilities between his own career and his controlling interest in the Collins Corporation.

Janet's children Liza and Gary are grown and on their own. Gary has followed in his father's footsteps with a career in medicine. Liza decided to marry Bruce Carson, but before that happened, she met Steve Kaslo. Her family felt that she might be marrying too young, but Liza was determined.

Things looked bright for the young couple, but it was discovered that Steve suffered from a form of leukemia and that only a bone-marrow transplant could save his life. The only compatible donor was Steve's sister, Amy. But Amy was pregnant and could not undergo the operation until after her child was born. As time ran out for Steve, Amy decided to have her child delivered early, in order to save her brother's life.

Steve recovered, but he had to take it easy. Stubborn and a strong believer in the man being the family provider, he was very upset when Liza began a modeling career. At first he refused to use Liza's money, but eventually she persuaded him to accept the fact that they could live a better life with her income.

Although he has reluctantly accepted things as they are, Steve still feels he is a failure. His masculinity is being threatened and he is overly jealous of Liza and her relationship with her manager, Woody Reid.

Liza, herself, is finally discovering that she is a complete

The similarities are amazing when you compare Mary Stuart to her character of Joanne Vincente.

woman and has a great deal of inner strength. She loves her career and does not want to give it up; at the same time, she is struggling to keep her marriage intact.

While Steve tries to make the best of his life, his sister, Amy, seems to be making the worst of hers. Highly sensitive and romantic, Amy fell head over heals in love with Bruce Carson, Jo Vincente's ward. When Amy discovered she was pregnant, she considered having an abortion but decided against it. When her daughter, Victoria, was born, Bruce tried to get her to marry him. But Amy wanted Bruce to marry her out of love, not from a sense of duty. Finally Amy relented, but only after she got Bruce to agree to an open marriage.

Bruce cares for his wife, but he is not in love with her. He has been trying to make the best of the situation, but because Amy has rejected his friendship and compassion, he has not been reticent about accepting out-of-town newspaper assignments.

While Bruce was away, Amy dreamed of his return, hoping that he would confess his love for her. But nothing changed. The chances for happiness for these two people would probably be greater if Amy would relent a little and if Bruce could show her some of the love he has given to his daughter.

Sadness seems to follow John Wyatt. His wife, Eunice, Jo's sister, was murdered by his former lover, Jennifer Pace Phillips. John and Eunice were happy until Jennifer, the perennial housewrecker, entered their lives.

In actuality, John's relationship with Jennifer was an innocent one, but Eunice, aware of Jennifer's reputation, became jealous and suspicious of her. This, coupled with Jennifer's scheming, brought about John and Eunice's separation.

Jennifer really loved John. When he returned to Eunice, Jennifer tried to commit suicide, believing that John would save her. When he wasn't at her side in the hospital, she began fantasizing John's presence and imagining that he wanted her to get rid of Eunice so that they could be together.

Jennifer's stepmother, Stephanie Pace, began to suspect that something was wrong with Jennifer. But whenever Stephanie would inquire, Jennifer would seem to come back to reality.

Jennifer followed Eunice for over a week in order to find the opportunity to keep what she believed was her promise to John: to kill Eunice. Meanwhile, John and Eunice, happily reconciled, were rebuilding their life together. John was just making plans to take Eunice on a holiday when Jennifer succeeded in murdering her. John, overcome by grief, determined to find out who destroyed his life and hired private investigator David Sloan.

Mary Stuart has played Joanne Barron since the show began. Like Jo, Mary has also been starting a second career for herself. Her songwriting, known to "Search" fans, has become a means of

Another twenty-five-year veteran of the show is Larry Haines, who plays Stu Bergman.

Stephanie Pace has lots of problems; Marie Cheatham, who plays her, takes life in stride.

118   THE SERIALS

communication for her, enabling her to reach her many fans as well as many young people in the country. On her concert tours, Mary tells her story in her songs. A divorcee, Mary is proud of her two grown children, Cynthia and Jeff. As Jo, Mary has watched the world change and her character grow and mature. Mary has matured, too, and enjoys being around young people.

When Larry Haines joined "Search" twenty-five years ago, his part as Stu Bergman was supposed to last for only a few weeks. But his natural flair for comedy attracted so much attention that the show's producer informed him that he had a job for life. Larry, a skilled comedian, began his serial career in radio. His talents also have been displayed on Broadway in musical comedy (he was nominated for a Tony for *Promises, Promises*), in films *(The Odd Couple),* and in TV commercial voiceovers. He appeared on nighttime television in "Maude." Larry also has the distinction of winning the 1975 Daytime Emmy Award as best actor. He and his wife, Gertrude, live in Connecticut with their daughter, Debbie.

Billie Lou Watt's character, Ellie Harper, is gentle, kind, and sensible. Billie Lou is gentle, kind, and effervescent. But where Ellie remained single until her union with Stu, Billie Lou has been happily married to actor Hal Studer and is the mother of two sons and a daughter. Once the voice of Astro Boy, Billie Lou has had a productive career on stage and television.

Peter Simon and Courtney Sherman are a rarity. They are married on the show and married in real life. Both are dedicated to their profession, but, unlike their characters of Scott and Kathy Phillips, they have proven that a working couple can have a happy home life. Peter is also a playwright and has had one of his plays produced off-Broadway. This second career takes up most of his spare time, but he always finds time to visit his three children by his

The oldest show on the air, "Search for Tomorrow," got everyone together for a cast shot. *From left:* Rick Lohman, Lewis Arlt, Billie Lou Watt, Val Dufour, Anne Wyndham, Joel Higgins, Mary Stuart, Michael Nouri, Larry Haines, Meg Bennett, Ann Williams, Morgan Fairchild, Courtney Sherman, Chris Lowe, Peter Simon, Drew Snyder.

It's too bad Joel Higgins doesn't get a chance to display his marvelous singing voice as Bruce Carson.

Delightful Billie Lou Watt plays equally delightful Ellie Bergman.

Happily married on both the show and in real life are Peter Simon and Courtney Sherman, who play Scott and Kathy Phillips.

John Cunningham and his wife, Carol, are just as happy as John's character of Wade Collins and his wife.

first marriage, Heather, Laura, and Matthew. Courtney feels that the serial affords her the best of two worlds. She can work at her chosen profession and still have plenty of time for her young daughter, Brooke.

Fun-loving John Cunningham plays Wade Collins on "Search." A strong believer in family life and involvement in local community projects, John, his wife, Carol, and their three children, Christopher, Cathy, and Laura, live in upstate New York, right behind the country club. Although John is not in politics, he believes in supporting the candidate of his choice. In his spare time, he enjoys boating and improving his house. One of Broadway's favorite stars, John particularly enjoyed playing John Adams in the musical *1776*. He is a direct descendant of Adams.

The home life of Millee Taggart, who plays Janet Bergman Walton, is one of warmth and humor. She met her husband, Barry Kurtz, when he sold her some insurance and she had to collect on it after a mishap in an aquatic dance show. At home, Millee's time is somewhat divided. She has her children, Matthew and Heather, her community affairs, and still runs her home. But her family is most important. Millee jokes that since her husband, Barry, appeared on the game show "Tattletales" with her, he is thinking of leaving the investment business for a career in the theater.

Tall, dark, and handsome may sound trite, but it is the only way to describe Michael Nouri, who portrays Steve. Michael has been concentrating on his songwriting, which he has displayed on the show, and is planning a record in the future. Unlike Steve, Michael encourages his wife, photographer Lynn Goldsmith, in her career. Mike is a warm, loving person, greatly concerned with the world and its people.

Vivacious Meg Bennett, who plays Liza Kaslo, found quick success in the theater. Beginning as a model, tall, willowy Meg has had experience in musicals, although she admits she never had professional training. Her long brown hair was covered up by a wig for her role in the Broadway show *Grease*, a role she had to give up when she joined "Search." She is well aware of the need for good nutrition and is generally a vegetarian. Her hobby? Collecting giraffes.

A gypsy at heart, Anne Wyndham has brought a gypsy quality to her gentle character of Amy. Anne is a gentle soul and somewhat of a "flower child," which makes you want to protect her. But she is also a strong person and has been on her own for many years. She first joined the daytime drama world on "General Hospital."

Unlike his character of Bruce, Joel Higgins is vibrant, bouncy, and great with the one-liners. Twice as handsome in person as he appears on TV, Joel enjoys his bachelor status. He always

A good mother, Millee Taggart poses with her TV son, Rick Lohman, and his real wife, Lenore.

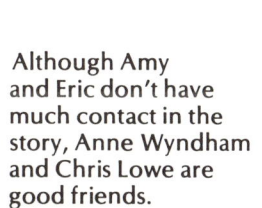

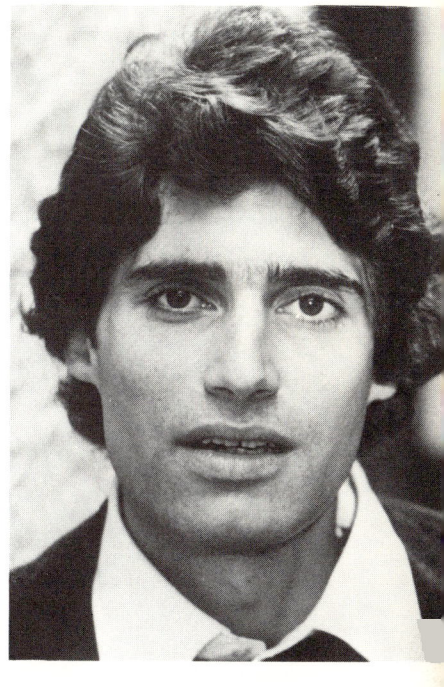

Michael Nouri often composes the songs he sings on the show as Steve Kaslo.

Although Amy and Eric don't have much contact in the story, Anne Wyndham and Chris Lowe are good friends.

Meg Bennett has modeled, just like her character, Liza.

Search for Tomorrow 121

Getting himself out of a murder charge has been a sticky problem for John Wyatt (Val Dufour).

seems to be doing two jobs at once; Broadway musicals are his second theatrical home.

How someone could portray a character as neurotic as Jennifer and be so well adjusted in real life is a question you might like to ask Morgan Fairchild. Morgan, a Texan, was born Patsy McClenny. She took the name Morgan from the movie of the same name, and a close friend suggested Fairchild. Morgan's career began in her home town, where her mother encouraged her to act to overcome her shyness. Morgan was Faye Dunaway's stand-in in the movie *Bonnie and Clyde,* and she has dated actors Warren Beatty, Telly Savalas, and Barry Newman. Morgan loves plants and is a strong believer in astrology; her mother often consults Morgan's chart for her.

A woman looking out for herself, yet a good mother and gentle at heart, is how you might describe Stephanie Pace. The actress who plays her, Marie Cheatham, is more sentimental and has stronger family roots. To keep herself close to her Texas upbringing, Marie has mementos from her grandparents' ranch proudly displayed on the walls of her Manhattan apartment. Needlepoint keeps Marie occupied in her spare moments, and she also collects Indian rugs and baskets. Religion is important to Marie, but it is also something that is very personal. Divorced, she has no children.

How can you describe Val Dufour, who plays John Wyatt, other than warm, happy, and full of fun? Divorced and the father of two grown children, Val is now a confirmed bachelor who enjoys escorting the ladies around town. Val knew poverty in his childhood, but he has managed to become one of the few millionaire actors. But because of his background, he admits to being exceptionally frugal today.

PART III
BEYOND THE SOAP SUDS

18 A Day in the Life of a Soap

Daytime serials have one thing in common: they produce a full show every day, five days a week, fifty-two weeks a year. Each working day, the actors follow the same schedule: they arrive at the studio; rehearse; have their hair, makeup, and wardrobe attended to; and tape a complete show.

Starting hour for the actors is usually 8:00 A.M. Other members of the show's personnel have already begun preparing for the day's activities.

The first stop for the actors is the rehearsal hall, where the day's script is read. Chairs and tables are arranged to represent the sets that they will be working with. The directors instruct each actor on where to sit, when to move, and so on. And it is not unusual for actors to make suggestions of their own. Dialogue may change somewhat, or actors may have their own feelings about movements and character reactions. This is the creative process at work—everyone pulling together to bring you the best possible show.

Early morning rehearsals are held in a large room with just tables and chairs, as in this one, where Nancy Addison, Ron Hale, and Michael Levin are taking a break.

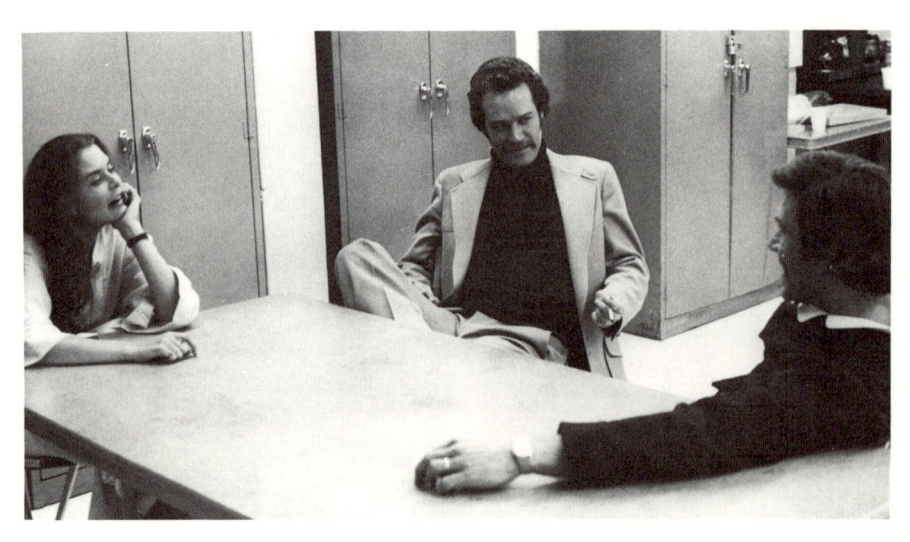

BEYOND THE SOAP SUDS

After they finish in the rehearsal hall, the actors usually head for their dressing rooms or to makeup and hairdressing. The process of turning themselves into their characters begins. It is amazing to watch this transformation as the day progresses.

Next stop is the studio, for camera blocking. Here the actors work with their sets, although not all the props are necessarily in place. Cameramen and sound men learn where the actors are to go and what types of shots are required. Here they discover if there is any difficulty in executing their movements. Once they are actually on the set, the actors may again make a few changes in dialogue or movement.

Dixie Carter listens to instructions from the director as she is put through her paces.

Choosing the wardrobe for the day is the job of the costume designer, but David Ackroyd browses through the racks of clothing for fun.

At this stage, the actresses often have their hair in rollers and their makeup half on. They are usually still in their street clothes. Quite often you will see actors carrying their scripts. This is not to study their lines, but because they have marked their scripts with their different movements and the times they are required to make them. The script is now a reference guide.

Back to the dressing rooms, for final makeup and hair comb-out. And for more study of the script. It is unusual to see anyone put a script aside. Actors like to make sure they are letter perfect on their lines. They take their work seriously, and this attention is reflected in the programs.

Now for a run-through where, hopefully, everything will work out as planned. The timing of the show is most important, and this task is usually left to the production assistant. She or he will have a stopwatch going during most of the rehearsals, letting the director and producers know if the show is running longer (or shorter) than the scheduled amount of time. If the time is long, director and producers get together and decide what material can be cut from the script. If the show is running short, the actors must adjust their movements and take more time delivering their lines.

Note-taking sessions usually take place after each rehearsal. The director gets together with the actors and lets them

A Day in the Life of a Soap

During a break on the set actors can often be found studying their scripts. Here are Charita Bauer, Fran Myers (who is also fixing her hair), and Don Stewart.

Run-through is when the cameras and actors work together for the first time; it is very important, as Mandy Kramer knows.

Between dress rehearsal and taping is the time a director gives notes to the actors. David Gale and Ann Flood listen carefully.

know how he would like them to change their delivery, or possibly where they should delay a movement or do it sooner. The producers may want something done differently, too, and the director relays their messages to the actors.

Most shows take their lunch break between the run-through and the dress rehearsal. This, of course, varies with the show and depends largely on whether a show is more than half an hour long.

Dress rehearsal is just that. Everything is performed as if it were the show to be taped. This is the most important preparatory time. Only in special cases are actors not fully dressed and made up for the show.

A break takes place between dress rehearsal and taping the show. Last-minute touchups are done, and final notes are given to the cast. Tension in the studio, which has been mounting all day, reaches its peak now. One most important observation. Unlike many other media, in which scenes are taped over and over, each serial tries to do its scenes only once. Of course, a major mishap or an equipment breakdown means the scene must be reshot. Daytime actors are adept at reshooting a scene; they can hit the same emotional level on the second try.

126   BEYOND THE SOAP SUDS

Waiting for the director to arrive and give them his notes are Victoria Wyndham, Will Lyman, and Fred Beir.

After the show is taped, everyone must wait for about fifteen minutes while the tapes are quickly reviewed and "cleared." Once clearance is announced, the actors are free to go home.

A few shows still have what is called a "pre-rehearsal." In this case, the actors involved in the next day's show go to the rehearsal hall and read through the script. Here they can change their dialogue or discuss why a character is reacting a certain way.

As we said in the beginning, every show is slightly different from every other. Most of the half-hour shows complete their day around 4:00 P.M. Then the actors go home, often to start studying for the next day's show.

"As the World Turns" tapes a show in two sections. Half the script is taped in the morning, the other half in the afternoon. (This show usually wraps up the day's shooting around 8:00 P.M.) Quite often the actors work only half a day, but even that is hard work.

"One Life to Live," a forty-five-minute show, works from 7:30 in the morning until 6:00 at night; "Days of Our Lives" puts in a 6:00 A.M. to 6:00 P.M. day. "Another World" follows a schedule that requires the actors to remain in the studio until 6:00 P.M.

Part of the day is covered by ABC press representative Jim Raftery, as he checks out what's new with Malcolm Groome.

A Day in the Life of a Soap

There are times during the day when actors can fool around. Susan Harney, Jacqueline Brooks, Barry Jenner, and Cathy Greene found time between dress rehearsal and the note session to have a hot game of ping-pong.

Dress rehearsal is most important, for it is performed exactly as if the show were on the air. John Driver and Lois Kibbee await their cues.

Note the microphone used in this scene with Forrest Compton. The cameramen must be careful not to have the mike show in the shot.

128   BEYOND THE SOAP SUDS

All those apartments and homes are actually just flats held up by 2 × 4s, as you can see in this scene between Tony Craig and Dixie Carter.

Five minutes before taping. The actors gather to go over their lines together or concentrate on their parts alone.

The makeup room is always crowded as actors vie for space to make repairs and get ready for the cameras.

A Day in the Life of a Soap   129

The finished products: scenes from ABC's "General Hospital" and "Ryan's Hope."

130   BEYOND THE SOAP SUDS

Tony Craig shows off the "crawl," which has all the credits for the day listed on it. You see it roll by on the screen at the end of the program.

The day is long and tiresome. The actors work hard to bring their characters to life and make the stories interesting. And a lot of other people work with them to make this possible: the writers, who develop the stories that keep audiences coming back for more; the stagehands and technicians, who try to make the actors' jobs easier and keep them looking beautiful before the cameras; the directors, who make suggestions and make the script come to life; and the producers, who handle problems and get everything to jell.

It is not easy to make a soap. Many people have tried and failed. But to those who have succeeded, who have made us hate or love them, who are in front of the cameras or behind the scenes—we offer a round of well-deserved applause.

A Day in the Life of a Soap

19
They Are More Than Soap Stars

To say that all actors and actresses excel in other phases of the arts is a sweeping generalization. Yet it is the exception rather than the rule for a performer not to possess some pretty fair credentials in several artistic capacities.

Daytime actors are among the most talented artists in their professions. Thus it is not unusual to find many serialists who have enormously successful second careers. Some have worked hard to achieve success in their "other" career, and for some, a new career "just happened."

Lovely Mary Stuart's success story is as fantastic as some of the problems she has faced as Joanne Barron Tate Vincente on "Search for Tomorrow." By the way, since that show made its debut on September 3, 1951, Mary has appeared on more hours of television than any performer in the world!

But, as she relates it, "I never intended to have an acting career—all I'd ever wanted to be was a singer. Around the age of twelve, I toured on the road with Bob Wills and His Texas Playboys. Later I went to Hollywood as a singer. Music producers and recording companies told me I didn't look the way I sounded. I should think not! I was only seventeen, but I had this low, sexy voice. So I ended up dubbing voices for other people, and they had someone else dub mine—a cute little soprano."

Today, nobody stifles Mary's rich, velvety smooth vocalizing. She's working on her second record album and sings and plays the guitar on nationwide concert tours that are especially popular on the college circuit.

But Mary Stuart's musical talent does not end there. Her sensitive lyrics, original music, and brilliant arrangements have been applauded by the critics. Former Beatle George Harrison says that he considers Mary Stuart to be one of the best songwriters on the scene today.

You may have heard a few of Mary's compositions on "Search for Tomorrow" and not have realized it. She wrote the

Mary Stuart sings and composes her own songs.

BEYOND THE SOAP SUDS

Christmas selections sung annually on the serial, and she also penned the memorable "Green Coffee," the lovers' theme employed during the Joanne Vincente-Sam Reynolds romance.

Another popular attraction on the concert circuit and in nightclubs is Don Stewart of "Guiding Light." Women loved him in his Mike Bauer role, but once the females across the nation discovered that they could hear Don's rich baritone in person, his cross-country appearances became sellouts.

Don displayed his acting and singing talents as Sir Lancelot in the Broadway musical *Camelot* and often appears in regional and summer stock productions. Every time his "Guiding Light" contract comes up for renewal, he considers leaving the show to devote his full time to music. But judging from his success at juggling two careers, Don Stewart will be around as Springfield's favorite lawyer for a while longer.

Ruth Warrick starred on Broadway in *Irene*, has been enormously successful in such movie classics as *Citizen Kane*, and plays Phoebe Tyler on "All My Children." But there were other fields to conquer.

In 1976 Ruth opened a Manhattan nightclub, called Top of the I. She wowed audiences with her vocal flair and style. Her musical parody of her character on "All My Children," which was written especially for her, was a tremendous hit. When asked why she decided to embark on a new career, Ruth said that she had always wanted to be a singer; it was a dream come true.

Craig Huebing, Dr. Peter Taylor on "General Hospital," is not a singer. But he recently became a published author with the release of his book of poems, *Daylight Moons*. He's currently working on another project. Craig is illustrating a book of children's stories being written by actress Victoria Shaw, who formerly played Kira Falkner on "General Hospital."

For two of the handsome leading men on "The Young and the Restless," singing is an important part of their careers. Beau Kayzer, who portrays Brock Reynolds, has released his first full-length record album, "Touch that Feeling," and co-star John McCook is a regular on the nightclub scene.

Beau's album features ten selections: five standards and five original tunes, including the beautiful "Young and Restless" theme, which is also known as "Nadia's Theme." Beau collaborated on the original songs with a good friend, composer Ben Weisman, who also wrote some of Elvis Presley's biggest hits. Beau is in the process of assembling a nightclub act and is also set to hit the talk-show circuit to publicize this latest venture.

John McCook sang and danced for his supper for several years before he entered the acting end of the business. In fact, he was a singer when he met his wife, actress-singer-dancer Juliet Prowse. John occasionally sings on the daytime drama and was re-

Nightclubs and Broadway have been the second home for Don Stewart.

Ruth Warrick finally fulfilled her dream of being a chanteuse.

Poetry is the second pursuit of Craig Huebing.

They Are More Than Soap Stars   133

Left:
Beau Kayzer is surrounded by the men who made his recent album possible.

Right:
Las Vegas has seen John McCook many times; he performs there with his wife, Juliet Prowse.

Janice Lynde has appeared on Broadway; now she hopes to ready a nightclub act to display her singing and dancing prowess.

cently featured in the afternoon musical extravaganza "After Hours, From Janice, John, Mary and Michael, With Love." The other three daytime actor-singers of the show's title were Mary Stuart, Michael Nouri, and Janice Lynde.

Growing up in New York, Janice entertained dreams of becoming a concert pianist. Endless hours of practice paid off handsomely, and today she is as skilled at the keys as she is in her acting. Not surprisingly, talented Janice is working on her first record album, and she has also been assembling a Las Vegas nightclub act.

The fourth member of that musical special, Michael Nouri, frequently delights "Search for Tomorrow" audiences with his heart-rending ballads and guitar playing. He has recorded the hit single "Daisies" and is putting together an album of his original compositions.

For the past fifteen years, Eileen Fulton has portrayed Lisa Miller Hughes Shea Colman on "As the World Turns." She is daytime's most memorable villainess. But Eileen is also a fine singer, and in 1976 she made her nightclub debut in Manhattan's elegant Persian Room in the Plaza Hotel. The engagement had been carefully planned to coincide with the release of Eileen's album, "For All Time," produced by her husband, recording executive Danny Fortunato.

In any discussion of daytime actors who have established successful musical careers, the name of Bill Hayes (Doug Williams on "Days of Our Lives") is a must. From his solos at his nightclub on the show, Doug's Place, viewers must know that Bill has had experience in the music industry.

Prior to moving to the West Coast, Bill lived in New York and starred on the classic "Your Show of Shows" with Sid Caesar, Imogene Coca, Carl Reiner, and Howard Morris. His "Ballad of

BEYOND THE SOAP SUDS

Davy Crockett" topped *Billboard*'s charts and sold in the millions! In the fall of 1976 Bill recorded his second album, "From Me to You with Love," a collection of twelve romantic ballads, backed by full orchestrations.

Another featured vocalist at Doug's Place on "Days of Our Lives" is the character of Trish Clayton, played by Patty Weaver. Thanks to her fans' persistent requests, former rock singer Patty completed her first solo album last year, "Patty Weaver Sings . . . As Time Goes By." The two guiding forces behind the project were famed arranger and jazz guitarist Mundell Lowe and Patty's husband, Larry Stewart, who served as executive producer since he heads her recording label, RE/SE Records. Larry says that the name of his record company stands for "round eyes/slant eyes." Patty's second album, "Feelings," should also be a big success.

One of Patty's background singers on the album is her very close friend from "Mary Hartman, Mary Hartman," Mary Kay Place. The popularity of Mary Kay's/Loretta Haggars' music, which Mary Kay writes most of, has blossomed into a successful music career for this young super-talent. During the summer of 1976, she worked on her first album for Columbia Records, with help from such artists as Emmylou Harris and Anne Murray. The entire production was done as Loretta Haggars and provided valuable experience for Mary Kay's next project: a second album as Mary Kay Place!

Another highly successful facet of Mary Kay Place is her writing expertise. She has co-authored scripts for popular series such as "Phyllis," "Rhoda," and "Maude."

John Gabriel's singing career began before he became an actor. Only recently, though, have the fans of "Ryan's Hope" become aware of his magnificent voice. He captured them with his rendition of "Gillian's Song" on that show.

John has been under contract to the recording divisions of United Artists and 20th Century-Fox. He has also had his own syndicated TV show, "Good Company," on which he sang and conducted interviews. And he was the vocalist who set the scene for such comedy acts as Joan Rivers, Phyllis Diller, and Stiller and Meara. Another sideline to his music was collaboration with Nelson Riddle. Riddle wrote the music to John's lyrics for the movies *El Dorado* and *The Fakers*.

John now has his own nightclub act, featuring music that is "close to me." He likes to say things with his music, and his act includes songs about love, marriage, kids, lost love, and the like. Most of the songs he sings are ones he wrote himself. He has hopes of taking his act on tour.

Watch out for daytimers—they're a bundle of talented surprises!

Besides his two recent albums, Bill Hayes has a gold record in his past.

Patty Weaver's two record albums have been great successes, as fans of her show well know.

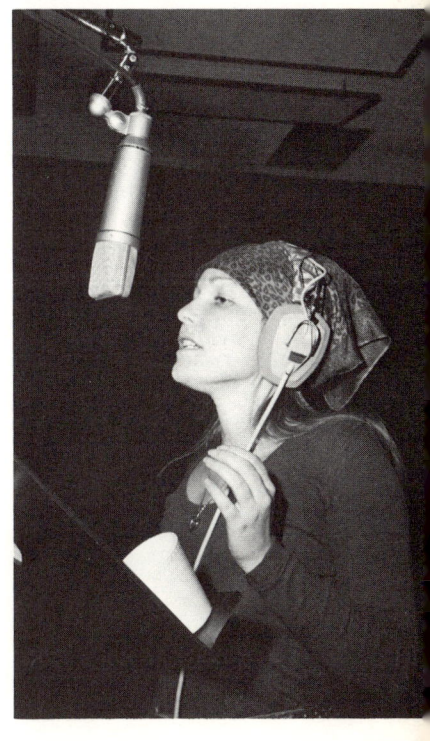

They Are More Than Soap Stars

20 The Famous Graduates

Daytime drama is one of the hardest acting jobs to master. Yet actors who have never performed in a soap either have great respect for their fellow thespians because they realize it is so hard, or they put down a medium that they know nothing about. The latter view is a pity, since a number of excellent Hollywood actors have tried serials and quit them because the pressure is so great.

Of the thousands of actors who have done soaps in the last thirty years, many have attained the status of star. Whether they are grateful for the experience they gained in front of the television camera or not does not matter. They gained the experience there and that is what is important.

Among the most famous daytime graduates is Warren Beatty, who was on "Love of Life" in the 1950s when the show was still telecast live. Beatty was then a struggling actor. He played the son of the man who owned the TV station for which "Love of Life's" heroine, Vanessa, worked.

"Love of Life" and "Search for Tomorrow" have two of the largest alumni rolls of all the serials. Peter Falk is a "Love of Life" graduate. He played a "heavy" during the 1950s, and although the name of his character has been lost, "L.O.L" director Larry Auerbach has kinescopes of some of the episodes in which Falk appeared.

Two actresses who have always given credit to "Love of Life" for helping them develop their skills are Jessica Walter and Bonnie Bedelia. Jessica, to this day, is occasionally recognized as her serial character, Julie Murano. Bonnie played Sandy Porter.

Don Knotts almost retired from acting when his role of the deaf-mute Wilbur Peabody ended on "Search for Tomorrow." Steve Allen rescued him, and the rest is history. Lee Grant and Nita Talbot both played Don's sister, Rose, during the 1950s.

Many of today's stars worked on the soaps when they were starting out in the business. Their roles weren't big, often just extras or small speaking parts. Dustin Hoffman did this type of work on "The Edge of Night" and "Search for Tomorrow." Jimmy Coco

In the early 1950s Warren Beatty performed on "Love of Life."

Peter Falk played a heavy on "Love of Life," and there are still some kinescopes of his performances around.

worked the same way on the same shows. "The Wild, Wild West's" Ross Martin was a frequent actor on "Search for Tomorrow" in small parts. Sandy Duncan was also on "Search."

Before "Route 66," George Maharis played Budd Gardner on "Search for Tomorrow." What would "The Fonz" do without Marion Cunningham and her tender care? Marion Ross, who plays Marion Cunningham, was Mary Morgan on "Paradise Bay." Donna McKechnie has been dancing up a storm and winning awards for her part in *A Chorus Line,* but she wasn't dancing in her dual roles of Amanda Harris and Olivia Cole on "Dark Shadows."

Although "One Man's Family" was one of radio's most famous and successful daytime soaps, it was broadcast at night on television. Tony Randall played Mac and Eva Marie Saint played Claudia Barbour. Eva Marie also played on "The Edge of Night" and "Young Dr. Malone."

Patty Duke Astin was just a child when she was on "A Brighter Day" and playing Molly Scharf on "Kitty Foyle." More famous people from "Brighter Day" are Lois Nettleton, Jack Lemmon, and Hal Holbrook. Hal played Grayling Dennis.

Two people whose careers were reactivated, and one whose career was given a boost, after their stints on "The Secret Storm" are Diane Ladd, Troy Donahue, and Cliff de'Young. Diane played Kitty Styles, Donahue was the maniac Keefer, and de'Young was Alden.

Ellen MacRae was excellent as Dr. Kate Bartok on "The Doctors." But that was before she won an Oscar and a Tony. You don't know Ellen MacRae? Today she's known as Ellen Burstyn. Who would Hutch be without Starsky? Paul Michael Glaser was known as Michael Glaser when he played Dr. Chernak on "Love Is a Many-Splendored Thing" and Dr. Joe Corelli on "Love of Life."

Carl Betz was on "Love of Life" as Collie Jordan before he traveled to Hollywood. And Robert Alda also did his part on that serial as Jason Ferris. Archie Bunker's zany wife, Edith, wasn't so zany when Jean Stapleton played Gwen on "Woman With a Past." And would you believe that Ted Knight appeared on a soap? He was on "Clear Horizon."

Before Cary Grant, before movie stardom, and even be-

Left:
Another "Love of Life" graduate is Jessica Walter.

Center:
Dustin Hoffman played bit parts on many serials before his success in *The Graduate.*

Right:
Jimmy Coco was a frequent player on "Search for Tomorrow" and "The Edge of Night."

George Maharis played Bud Gardner on "Search for Tomorrow."

The Famous Graduates 137

Tony Randall's experience with soaps goes back to the 1950s.

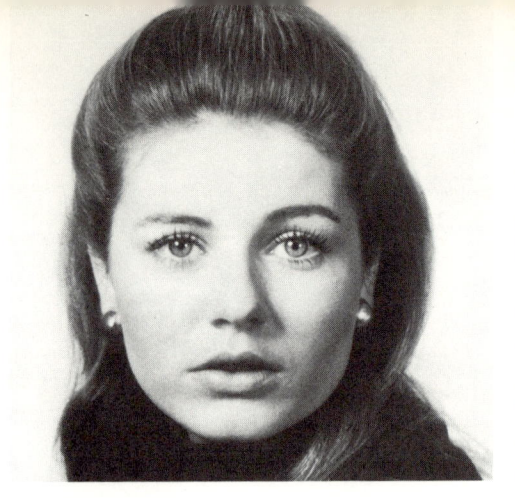

Patty Duke Astin performed as a child on several soaps.

Jack Lemmon did not get a chance to display his comedy talents on the serials.

When she was known as Ellen MacRae, Ellen Burstyn played Dr. Kate Bartok on "The Doctors."

"Full Circle" was the start of Dyan Cannon's career.

Richard Thomas was just a toddler when he was on "As the World Turns."

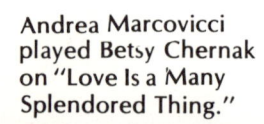

Andrea Marcovicci played Betsy Chernak on "Love Is a Many Splendored Thing."

It was a long time ago and before her Hollywood career that Diana Muldaur was on "The Secret Storm."

Would you believe Efrem Zimbalist, Jr. on a serial?

fore she spelled her name with a Y, Dyan Cannon starred on "Full Circle" in the part of Lisa Crowder.

When he was much younger and long before he became John-Boy, Richard Thomas did many serials, including "A Time for Us," "From These Roots," and "As the World Turns." He played Tommy Hughes on "World." Just coming into her due as a star is Andrea Marcovicci, Woody Allen's leading lady in *The Front*. Andrea played Betsy Chernak on "Love Is a Many-Splendored Thing." Other "Splendored Thing" graduates include David Birney, who was Mark Elliott, and Donna Mills, who played Laura Elliott.

Diana Muldaur's movie and television career has been booming since she was Ann Wicker on "The Secret Storm." Both Roy Scheider and Tony LoBianco were on "Hidden Faces." Scheider went on to many serials, including "Search for Tomorrow" as Dr. Wheeler and "Love of Life" as Jonas Falk. LoBianco also appeared on "Love of Life," playing Dr. Joe Corelli.

Dana Andrews starred in "Bright Promise" as Professor Thomas Boswell. And Efrem Zimbalist, Jr., played Jim Gavin on "Concerning Miss Marlowe."

Nighttime situation comedies have become the home for many former daytime stars. Conrad Bain of "Maude" was Dr. Facciola on "Search for Tomorrow," and Rue McClanahan was Margaret Jordas on "Where the Heart Is." Rue also played the menacing Caroline on "Another World." Hal Linden once played Larry Carter on "Search for Tomorrow" and David Groh was the "heavy" JoJo on "The Edge of Night." J. A. Preston (known as James in his serial days) was on "Another World" as Raymond Scott. And Esther Rolle got her early TV experience as Sadie Gray on "One Life to Live."

The soap experiences of Jane Rose go all the way back to when soaps began on TV. She was Sarah Dale on "Love of Life," Becky Winkle on "Somerset," and Aggie Parsons on "The Secret Storm." Patty McCormack may have played a "bad seed" as a child, but as an adult she was Linda Warren on "The Best of Everything." Geraldine Fitzgerald also starred on "The Best of Everything," as Violet Jordan. And distinguished actress Gale Sondergaard played Amanda Kay on it. Ms. Sondergaard also appeared on "Ryan's Hope," as Marguerite Beaulac.

Beautiful Kate Jackson recalls her happy years as Daphne Harridge on "Dark Shadows." And Trish Van Devere did two soaps in her early career. She played Patti Tate on "Search for Tomorrow" and Meredith Wolek on "One Life to Live." Sandy Dennis also experienced the soaps for a day on "The Guiding Light."

Both Tony Roberts and Larry Hagman got good starts on "The Edge of Night." Tony played Lee Pollack, and Larry was Ed Gibson. Delicately featured Joanna Pettet made a good beginning as Judy Stratton on "The Doctors."

Rue McClanahan was not a nice character when she was on "Another World."

David Groh played a hood named JoJo on "The Edge of Night."

Jane Rose's daytime career dates back to early television.

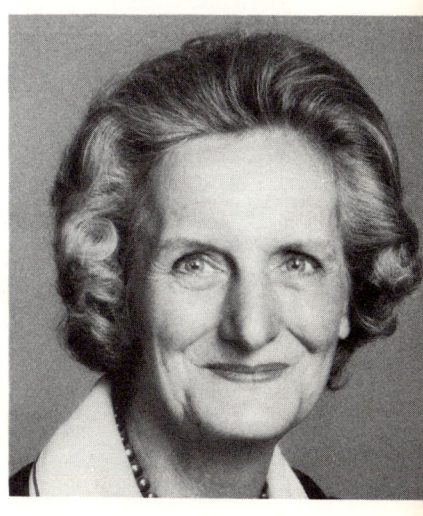

The Famous Graduates

Do you remember when Jill Clayburgh played Grace Bolton on "Search for Tomorrow"? Or when Richard Hatch captured all the girls' hearts when he was Phil Brent (the original) on "All My Children"? Perhaps you can recall when Wayne Rogers was under contract to "Search for Tomorrow." Or the marvelous Gerald S. O'Laughlin when he played Pete Banas on "The Doctors."

On his nighttime show, Barry Newman was always making sure his name, Petrocelli, was pronounced correctly. But on "The Edge of Night" his name was much simpler: John Barnes. Anyone who watches "Days of Our Lives" feels only compassion for Laura Horton. Susan Flannery, who played Laura for several years, went on to fame in *The Towering Inferno*. Wonder how it felt to kiss Robert Wagner?

Charles Durning stayed on "Another World" for only a short time, as Gil McGowan, but Audra Lindley's role of Liz Matthews lasted much longer. Bettye Ackerman played Constance McKenzie for a year on "Return to Peyton Place," and Marsha Mason went on to stage and movie fame after her Judy Cole role on "Love of Life" ended.

All these people brought their own special brand of magic to the shows. Now, whenever someone puts down soaps, you can say, "But didn't you know so-and-so started in them?" Soap opera is an important part of the entertainment medium not only to the viewers at home, but also to the stars of the future.

Left:
After winning success in "The Bad Seed," Patty McCormack starred on "The Best of Everything."

Right:
Before nightclubs, game shows, and movies, Bert Convy performed on "Love of Life."

140 BEYOND THE SOAP SUDS

Top left:
There are several serial roles in Trish Van Devere's past, including ones in "Search for Tomorrow" and "One Life to Live."

Top right:
Sandy Dennis's daytime experience on The "Guiding Light" lasted only one day.

Center:
"Petrocelli" was a good man, but Barry Newman as John Barnes on "The Edge of Night" wasn't.

Bottom left:
"M*A*S*H" has been successful for Mike Farrell, but that followed his stint on "Days of Our Lives."

Bottom right:
Although Edward Winter was a questionable character on "Somerset," his role on "M*A*S*H" is lots of fun.

Cecily Tyson and James Earl Jones played husband and wife Jim and Martha Frazier on "The Guiding Light." James was on "As the World Turns" as Dr. Jerry Turner, too. And Billy Dee Williams was the assistant district attorney on "Another World."

Dancing was the start of Zina Bethune's career, but an injury turned her to acting. She played Robin Holden on "The Guiding Light" and Barbara Latimore on "Love of Life." Through exercise and practice, Zina is once again dancing, her first love.

Often playing the villain today in movies and nighttime shows, Patrick O'Neal was on "Portia Faces Life" and "Today Is Ours," in which he played Karl Manning. Comedian Dick Van Patten's role on "Young Dr. Malone" wasn't anywhere near funny. And Lee Merriweather did several serials after winning her Miss America title. She played Nora on "Clear Horizon" and Ann Reynolds on "The Young Marrieds."

Wicked witches are behind Margaret Hamilton; since then she has been staid secretary Mrs. Peterson on "As the World Turns." Teen-agers Robby Benson and Glynnis O'Connor worked the soaps. Robby was the original Bruce Carson on "Search for Tomorrow," and Glynnis was Dawn Stewart on "As the World Turns."

Zina Bethune played Barbara Latimer on "Love of Life" for many years.

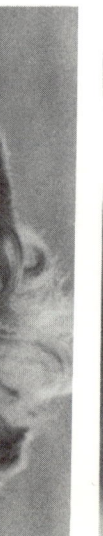

Now a great comedian, Dick Van Patten has worked the serials several times.

Robby Benson had to leave his role of Bruce Carson on "Search for Tomorrow" to fulfill a movie contract.

142   BEYOND THE SOAP SUDS

After the "Lassie" films, Tommy Rettig played JoJo on "Never Too Young." When he grew up and left "Leave It to Beaver" behind, Tony Dow played Ross Jeanelle on "General Hospital." "The Jeffersons" are Damon Evans' family now, but he was once on "Love of Live." And the former Loretta Allen of "Love of Life," Ja'net DuBois, is finding nothing but "Good Times."

American Graffiti was a very popular movie. One of its stars, Cindy Carroll, played Susan on "Never Too Young." In the cast with her was Elinor Donahue of "Father Knows Best" and later, "The Odd Couple." Just a year after leaving "Another World" and her role of Lenore Curtin, Susan Sullivan found a home in "Rich Man, Poor Man, Book II."

The rugged good looks of Joseph Campanella were once seen on "The Guiding Light." And singer and game-show host Bert Convy had the role of Glen Hamilton on "Love of Life" in his early career. Being stereotyped as a doctor seems to follow Barnard Hughes around. He played Dr. Bruce Banning on "The Guiding Light" before he appeared in the movie *Hospital* and on the nighttime TV show "Doc."

Glynnis O'Connor first came to prominence as Dawn Stewart on "As the World Turns."

"Love of Life" graduate Ja'net DuBois is finding "Good Times" now.

Damon Evans was also a "Love of Life" graduate.

Susan Sullivan took a chance in leaving "Another World"; then she landed a role in "Rich Man, Poor Man, Book II."

The Famous Graduates   143

21 The Emmy Awards

Mary Fickett was the first actress to win an Emmy in daytime drama, for her role on "All My Children" in 1973.

Macdonald Carey won the daytime Emmy as Best Actor three years in a row (1973, 1974, and 1975), for his portrayal of Dr. Tom Horton on "Days of Our Lives."

It seems remarkable that in the more than twenty-five years that the National Academy of Television Arts and Sciences has been established, daytime serials have been recognized by the Emmy committee for only the last five years. True, through the efforts of her castmates, Mary Stuart of "Search for Tomorrow" was the first daytime actress nominated for an award, but she lost out. The members of the Academy probably did not know who she was. Daytime drama was still the stepchild of television. It was not taken seriously, and the actors on the shows were thought of as nonprofessionals.

But things are changing. Daytime drama was first given recognition during the 1973 Emmy telecast. Even then, the daytime awards were pushed aside and were the first ones cut by the Academy when time ran short. They managed to announce (in a hurried-up fashion) only the award given to "The Edge of Night" as the outstanding serial. Actress Mary Fickett of "All My Children" and actor Macdonald Carey of "Days of Our Lives" had to wait until the next day to learn that they had won awards.

By 1974 the daytime community had won the right to their own special, shown during the day and honoring the daytime people and the contributions that they make to television. After all, daytime drama goes a long way toward supporting the more expensive nighttime programming.

NBC hosted the first Daytime Emmy Awards ceremony. Excitement mounted as the multitudes gathered, many of them hoping to be among the winners. Once again, Macdonald Carey of "Days of Our Lives" was voted Best Actor. Elizabeth Hubbard was named Best Actress for her role of Althea Davis on "The Doctors."

"The Doctors" won the Best Serial award. The awards ceremony wasn't perfect, but it was an auspicious beginning.

In 1975, ABC produced the daytime Emmys and decided to do something spectacular. They held the ceremony on one of the Circle Line boats that cruises around Manhattan. As the boat weighed anchor in New York Harbor, near the Statue of Liberty, the balmy sea breezes offset the summer heat. In high spirits, the daytime actors, along with the viewing audience, eagerly anticipated the announcements of the winners. Already twice a winner, Macdonald Carey walked off with his third Best Actor award. And it was fitting that his co-star Susan Flannery, be given the Best Actress award on her retirement from "Days of Our Lives." For Susan, it was the start of a big year in her career. Later she won the Golden Globe as Most Promising Newcomer for her work in *The Towering Inferno*. Then, two years old and fast becoming one of the most popular soaps ever to hit the airwaves, "The Young and the Restless" won the Best Serial award.

For the first time in its history, Lincoln Center opened up the Vivian Beaumont Theater to television when CBS held the Third Annual Emmy Awards in 1976. The luncheon that precedes the program was held around the outdoor fountain, and fans gathered from all over to catch a glimpse of their favorite stars. With a more formal setting than in previous years, the daytime community now settled down to accepting the awards ceremony as a yearly event. Excitement was as high as ever, however, and winners were rousingly cheered.

Twenty-five-year veteran of "Search for Tomorrow" Larry Haines was voted Best Actor. Helen Gallagher of "Ryan's Hope" was awarded the Best Actress award. And the first serial to expand to an hourly format, "Another World," garnered the Best Serial prize.

With the Daytime Emmy Awards an annual event for three years now, it looks as if it is here to stay. There are some grumblings in the acting community about the format, but almost everyone is willing to work at it to give the full range of people involved in the serials their well-deserved acknowledgment.

Many of the actors have expressed the feeling that it is difficult to choose a Best Actor or Best Actress; in any given year there are too many variables to be considered. Stories start and peak, giving the many players on each soap a chance to display their skills. But as Erika Slezak of "One Life to Live" says, "Although the Emmys aren't perfect, they are the only way we have to commend the professionals in the daytime serial world."

Best daytime actress in 1975 was Susan Flannery, for her portrayal of Laura Horton on "Days of Our Lives." Here she's flanked by her former co-stars Ron Husmann and Wesley Eure.

Helen Gallagher ("Ryan's Hope") and Larry Haines ("Search for Tomorrow") won Emmys in 1976.

The Emmy Awards 145

APPENDIX
A Guide to All the Soaps That Ever Were

The televised serial has been around for over thirty years. Granted, the first show, "Big Sister," lasted only a single day and was seen only in Chicago. But that was 1946, and TV was still in its infancy. Irna Phillips, recognized as the founder of the radio serial, then wrote "These Are Our Children," which was again broadcast only in Chicago. But a good many serials have been on the air over the years. Here is a list of all the shows that have appeared, excluding those that are still running. The shows are arranged chronologically according to the year they began, listing their stars and when they were canceled.

1947

HIGHWAY TO THE STARS (Dumont). *Cast:* Flora Campbell, Ann Stell, Mel Brandt, Dorene Scott, Frederick Meyer, Hal Studer, Bill Gale, Jack Holloran, Vivian King, Julie Christy, Warren Stevens. *Canceled:* October 9, 1947.

A WOMAN TO REMEMBER (Dumont). *Cast:* Frankie Thomas, Joan Castle, John Raby, Ruth McDevitt, Pat Wheel. *Canceled:* 1949.

1949

ONE MAN'S FAMILY (NBC). *Cast:* Bert Lytell, Theodore Von Eltz, Marjorie Gateson, Mary Adams, Eva Marie Saint, Anne Whitfield, Tony Randall, Jim Boles, Madeline Bugard, Lilian Schaff, Linda Reighton, James Lee, Walter Brooke, Jack Edwards. *Canceled:* April 1, 1955.

THE O'NEILLS (Dumont). *Cast:* Vera Allen, Ian Martin, Celia Budkin, Ben Fishbern, Janice Gilbert, Michael Lawson, Jane West. *Canceled:* 1949.

THESE ARE MY CHILDREN (NBC). *Cast:* Jane Brooksmith, Joan Alt, George Luge, Eloise Kunner, Alma Platto. *Canceled:* 1949.

1950

FAIRMEADOWS, U.S.A. (NBC). *Cast:* Tom Tyler, Mimi Stragin, Howard St. John, Hazel Dawn, Ruth Matheson.

THE FIRST 100 YEARS (CBS). *Cast:* Larry Haines, Carl Low, Nat Polen, Nancy Malone, Robert Armstrong, James Lydon, Anne Sargent, Don Tobin, Valerie Cassort. *Canceled:* June 27, 1952.

HAWKINS FALLS, POPULATION 6200 (NBC). *Cast:* Frank Dane, Alice Dinsen, Sam Gray, Arthur Peterson, Hope Summers, Mary Desmond, Bill Snary, Bernadene Flynn. *Canceled:* 1952.

1951

THE EGG AND I (CBS). *Cast:* Patricia Kirkland, Carl Low, Grady Sutton, Frank Twedell, Doris Rich. *Canceled:* August 1, 1952.

MISS SUSAN (NBC). *Cast:* Louise Hallister, Anne Seymour, Maxine Stuart, Nancy Sheridan, Sallie Brophy. *Canceled:* 1954.

THE BENNETTS (NBC). *Cast:* Sam Gray, Ray Westfall, Jack Lester, Jerry Harvey, Don Gibson, Sam Siegel, Beverly Younger, Paula Houston. *Canceled:* January 8, 1954.

THREE STEPS TO HEAVEN (NBC). *Cast:* Lori March, Diana Douglas, Phyllis Hill, Kathleen McGuire, Mark Roberts, Laurie Vendig, Irving Taylor, Walter Brooke, Ginger McManus. *Canceled:* December 31, 1954.

1954

A TIME TO LIVE (NBC). *Cast:* Larry Kerr, Len Wayland, Jack Lester, Patricia Sully. *Canceled:* December 31, 1954.

CONCERNING MISS MARLOWE (CBS). *Cast:* John Gibson, Louise Albritton, Elaine Raust, Efrem Zimbalist, Jr., Jane Seymour, John Raby. *Canceled:* 1955.

THE BRIGHTER DAY (CBS). *Cast:* William Smith, Gloria Hoye, Forrest Compton, Abby Lewis, Del Hughes, Larry Ward, Patty Duke, Lois Nettleton, Hal Holbrook, Jack Lemmon, Lori March, Joe Sirola, Mona Bruns, Santos Ortega, Mary K. Wells, Sam Gray, Muriel Williams, Bill Post, Bob Hastings. *Canceled:* September 28, 1962.

FIRST LOVE (NBC). *Cast:* Patricia Barry, Val Dufour, Rosemary Prinz, Frederic Downs, Howard Smith, Jay Barney. *Canceled:* December 30, 1954.

THE GREATEST GIFT (NBC). *Cast:* Phillip Foster, Ann Burr. *Canceled:* September 28, 1954.

GOLDEN WINDOWS (NBC). *Cast:* Grant Sullivan, Eric Dressler, Herb Patterson, Leila Martin. *Canceled:* September 28, 1954.

PORTIA FACES LIFE (CBS). *Cast:* Fran Carlon, Frances Reid, Renne Jarrett, Patrick O'Neal, Charles Taylor, Ginger McManus, Karl Swenson. *Canceled:* March 11, 1955. (This serial was later known as "The Inner Flame.")

ROAD OF LIFE (CBS). *Cast:* Don MacLaughlin, Virginia Dwyer, Bill Lipton, Elspeth Eric, Jack Lemmon, Harry Holcombe, Dorothy Sands.

THE SECRET STORM (CBS). *Cast:* Lori March, Jada Rowland, Bernard Barrow, Warren Berlinger, Judy Lewis, Lynn Adams, Ward Costello, Barbara Rodell, Larry Block, Marla Adams, Jacqueline Brooks, Alexander Scourby, Linden Chiles, Nick Coster, Joel Crothers, Stephanie Braxton, Dan Hamilton, David Ackroyd, Diane Ladd, Marjorie Gateson, Eleanor Phelps, Bruce Sherwood, Robert Venture, Cliff de'Young, Troy Donahue, Diana Muldaur, Jennifer Darling, Mary K. Wells, Robert Loggia, Laurence Luckinbill, Virginia Dwyer, Charles Baxter, Keith Charles, Joan Hotchkiss. *Canceled:* February 15, 1974.

THE SEEKING HEART (CBS). *Cast:* Scott Forbes, Dorothy Lovett, Flora Campbell. *Canceled:* December 10, 1954.

WOMAN WITH A PAST (CBS). *Cast:* Constance Ford, Jean Stapleton, Barbara Myers, Ann Hegira. *Canceled:* July 2, 1954.

THE WORLD OF MR. SWEENEY (NBC). *Cast:* Charlie Ruggles, Helen Wagner, Betty Garde, Gene Walker, Janet Fox, Lydia Reed.

VALIANT LADY (CBS). *Cast:* Abby Lewis, Dolores Sutton, James Kirkwood, Flora Campbell, Nancy Coleman, Anne Pearson.

1955

A DATE WITH LIFE (NBC). *Cast:* Dolores Sutton, Barbara Britton, Anthony Eisley, Logan Field, Mark Roberts, June Dayton. *Canceled:* June 29, 1956.

WAY OF THE WORLD (NBC). *Cast:* Gloria Louis, Ann Burr, Addison Powell. *Canceled:* 1955.

1957

HOTEL COSMOPOLITAN (CBS). *Cast:* James Pritchett, Donald Woods, Henderson Forsythe, Walter Brooke, John Holmes. *Canceled:* April 11, 1958.

1958

FROM THESE ROOTS (NBC). *Cast:* Ann Flood, Susan Brown, Henderson Forsythe, Billie Lou Watt, Robert Mandan, Audra Lindley, Barbara Berjer, Millette Alexander, Craig Huebing, John Colenback, Vera Allen, Sam Gray, Gary Morgan. *Canceled:* 1962.

KITTY FOYLE (NBC). *Cast:* Kathleen Murray, Bob Hastings, Judy Lewis, Patty Duke, William Redfield, Conard Fowkes, Karl Weber, Les Damon. *Canceled:* June 27, 1958.

TODAY IS OURS (NBC). *Cast:* Ernest Graves, Patrick O'Neal, Patricia Benoit, Nancy Sheridan, Chase Crosley, Joanna Roos, Martin Blaine, Barry Thompson, Eugenia Rawls. *Canceled:* January 27, 1959.

YOUNG DR. MALONE (NBC). *Cast:* John Connell, William Prince, Virginia Dwyer, Augusta Dabney, Judson Laire, Lesley Woods, Lenka Peterson, Dick Van Patten, Zina Bethune, Eva Marie Saint, Joan Westmore, Kathleen Widdoes *Canceled:* December 29, 1961.

1959

FOR BETTER OR WORSE (CBS). *Cast:* James A. Peterson, William Wintersole, June Walker. *Canceled:* June 24, 1960.

THE HOUSE ON HIGH STREET (NBC). *Cast:* Philip Abbot, Enid Markey, Donald Madden, Judge James Gehrig, Harris B. Becker. *Canceled:* February 5, 1960.

1960

CLEAR HORIZON (CBS). *Cast:* Ed Kemmer, Phyllis Avery, Lee Merriweather, Richard Coogan, Ted Knight, Denise Alexander, Grace Albertson, Michael Cox, Jimmy Carter. *Canceled:* March 10, 1961. (This show returned March 8, 1962-June 11, 1962.)

FULL CIRCLE (CBS). *Cast:* Dyan Cannon, Robert Fortier, Michael Ross, Andrew Colman, Sam Edwards, John McNamara. *Canceled:* March 1, 1961.

ROAD TO REALITY (ABC). *Cast:* Eugenia Rawls, John Beal, Robert Drew, Judith Braun, Kay Doubleday. *Canceled:* March 31, 1961.

1962

DR. HUDSON'S SECRET JOURNAL (Syndicated). *Cast:* John Howard, Jean Howel, Frances Mercer.

OUR FIVE DAUGHTERS (NBC). *Cast:* Jacqueline Courtney, Ester Ralston, Patricia Allison, Wynne Miller, Nuella Dierking, Iris Joyce, Michael Keen. *Canceled:* September 28, 1962.

1963

BEN JERROD (NBC). *Cast:* Michael Ryan, Regina Gleason, Lyle Talbot, William Phillips, John Napier, Peter Hansen, Addison Richards. *Canceled:* June 28, 1963.

1964

THE YOUNG MARRIEDS (ABC). *Cast:* Peggy McCay, Susan Brown, Lee Merriweather, Susan Seaforth, Floy Dean, Paul Picerni, Michael Mikler, Ken Metcalf, Charles Grodin, Scott Graham, Brenda Benet, Frank Maxwell. *Canceled:* March 25, 1966.

1965

A TIME FOR US (ABC). *Cast:* Joanna Miles, Beverly Hayes, Richard Thomas, Lenka Peterson, Roy Poole, Kathleen Maguire, Conard Fowkes, Jacqueline Brooks, Jill O'Hara, Lynn Rogers, Frank Schofield, Robert Hogan, John McMartin. *Canceled:* December 16, 1966. (This show was originally titled "Flame in the Wind.")

MOMENT OF TRUTH (NBC). *Cast:* Douglass Watson, Louise King, Peter Donat, John Bethune, Ivor Barry, Sandra Scott, Chris Wiggins, Steven Levy, Lynne Gorman. *Canceled:* November 5, 1965.

MORNING STAR (NBC). *Cast:* Elizabeth Perry, Burt Douglas, Betty Lou Gerson, Olive Dunbar, Adrienne Ellis, Ed Prentiss. *Canceled:* July 1, 1966.

NEVER TOO YOUNG (ABC). *Cast:* Tommy Rettig, Tony Dow, Pat Connolly, Dack Rambo, John Lupton, David Watson, Michael Blodgett, Patrice Wymore. *Canceled:* June 24, 1966.

OUR PRIVATE WORLD (CBS). *Cast:* Eileen Fulton, Robert Drivas, Geraldine Fitzgerald, Nicolas Coster, David O'Brien, Sam Groom, Sandra Scott. *Canceled:* September 10, 1965. (This was the nighttime spinoff from "As the World Turns.")

PARADISE BAY (NBC). *Cast:* Keith Andes, Marion Ross, Heather North, Walter Brooke, Steve Mines. *Canceled:* July 1, 1966.

SCARLETT HILL (Syndicated). *Cast:* Ivor Barry, Ed McNamara, Alan Pearce, Beth Lockerbie, Lucy Warner.

THE NURSES (ABC). *Cast:* Mary Fickett, Melinda Plank, Leonie Norton, Nat Polen, Paul Stevens, Nicholas Pryor, Alan Feinstein. *Canceled:* March 31, 1967.

1966

DARK SHADOWS (ABC). *Cast:* Joan Bennett, Jonathan Frid, Alexandra Moltke, Nancy Barrett, Grayson Hall, Kathryn Leigh Scott, Lara Parker, Joel Crothers, David Selby, Roger Davis, David Ford, Clarice Blackburn, Anthony George, Denise Nickerson, Lisa Richards, Marie Wallace, Robert Rodan, Thayer David, Jerry Lacy, Donna McKechnie, Humbert Allen Astredo, Kate Jackson, Alan Feinstein. *Canceled:* April 2, 1971.

1967

LOVE IS A MANY SPLENDORED THING (CBS) *Cast:* Andrea Marcovicci, David Birney, Donna Mills, Leslie Charleson, Bibi Besch, Vincent Baggetta, Diana Douglas, Michael Hawkins, Gloria Hoye, Judson Laire, Edward Power, Leon Russom, Albert Stratton, Constance Towers, Stephen Joyce, Peter White, Paul Michael Glaser, Salome Jens, Barbara Stanger. *Canceled:* March 23, 1973.

1968

HIDDEN FACES (NBC). *Cast:* Conard Fowkes, Rita Gam, Louise Shaffer, Stephen Joyce, Roy Scheider, Gretchen Walther, Tony LoBianco. *Canceled:* June 30, 1969.

1969

BRIGHT PROMISE (NBC). *Cast:* Dana Andrews, Paul Lukather, Gail Kobe, Regina Gleason, Anne Jeffreys, Susan Brown, Dabney Coleman, John Considine, Tony Geary, Cheryle Miller, Mark Miller, Pamela Murphy, Lesley Woods, Ruth McDevitt, Nancy Stevens, Gary Pillar. *Canceled:* March 31, 1972.

STRANGE PARADISE (Syndicated). *Cast:* Colin Fox, Tudi Wiggins, Angela Roland, Dan McDonald, Bruce Gray, Patricia Collins, Trudy Young, Paisley Maxwell.

WHERE THE HEART IS (CBS). *Cast:* James Mitchell, Diana Walker, Gregory Abels, Diana van der Vlis, David Cryer, Bibi Osterwald, Janet League, Tracy Brooks Swope, Peter MacLean, Ted LePlatt, Rue McClanahan, Barbara Baxley, Zohra Lampert, Laurence Luckinbill, Ron Harper, Mason Adams, Jeanne Ruskin. *Canceled:* March 23, 1973.

1970

A WORLD APART (ABC). *Cast:* Susan Sarandon, Augusta Dabney, Susan Sullivan, Heather MacRae, William Prince, Roy Shuman, James Noble, Judith Barcroft, Robert Gentry, Elizabeth Lawrence. *Canceled:* June 25, 1971.

THE BEST OF EVERYTHING (ABC). *Cast:* Patty McCormack, Geraldine Fitzgerald, Gale Sondergaard, Barry Ford, Katherine Glass, Ted LePlatt, Julie Mannix, Terry O'Sullivan, Jane Alice Brandon, M'el Dowd. *Canceled:* September 24, 1970.

SOMERSET (NBC). *Cast:* Gloria Hoye, Michael Lipton, Jordan Charney, Ann Wedgeworth, Nicholas Coster, Dorothy Stinnette, Alice Hirson, Georgann Johnson, Len Gochman, Susan McDonald, Ron Martin, Renne Jarrett, Fawne Harriman, Edward Winter, Ernest Thompson, Bibi Besch, Jane Rose, Gretchen Wyler, Stanley Grover, Eleanor Phelps, Diahn Williams, Nancy Pinkerton, Dick Shoberg, Lois Smith, Audrey Landers. *Canceled:* December 31, 1976.

1971

OUR STREET (PBS). *Cast:* Barbara Mealy, Sandra Sharp, Arthur French, Janet League, Darryl F. Hill, Pat Picketts, Tyrone Jones, Frances Foster. *Canceled:* October 10, 1974.

1972

PAUL BERNARD, PSYCHIATRIST (Syndicated). *Cast:* Christopher Wiggins, Tudi Wiggins, Marcia Diamond, Shelley Sommers, Phyllis Maxwell, Gale Garnett, Paisley Maxwell, Arlene Meadows, Micki Moore, Dawn Greenhaigh.

RETURN TO PEYTON PLACE (NBC). *Cast:* Bettye Ackerman, Susan Brown, Warren Stevens, Katherine Glass, Frank Ferguson, Yale Summers, Lawrence Casey, Ron Russell, Lynn Loring, Julie Parrish, Patricia Morrow, Stacy Harris, Evelyn Scott, Guy Stockwell, Joe Gallison, Mary K. Wells, Ben Andrews, John Hoyt, Anne Seymour, Betty Ann Carr, Margaret Mason. *Canceled:* January 4, 1976.

1974

HOW TO SURVIVE A MARRIAGE (NBC). *Cast:* Rosemary Prinz, Joan Copeland, Jennifer Harmon, Lauren White, Elissa Leeds, Allan Miller, Fran Brill, Tricia O'Neil, Cathy Greene, James Shannon, Peter Brandon, George Welbes, Michael Landrum, Dino Narizzano, F. Murray Abraham, Armand Assante, Veleka Gray, Albert Ottenheimer, Al Fann, Gene Bua. *Canceled:* April 17, 1975.

Billie Lou Watt, as she appeared on "From These Roots."

Four of the stars from the short-lived "The Best of Everything" were Julie Mannix, Katherine Glass, Patty McCormack, and Rochelle Oliver.

"A World Apart" didn't last long, but it gave Susan Sarandon her start.

"Return to Peyton Place" had Joe Gallison and Mary Kay Wells as two of its stars.

Index

| c character | p producer |
| a actor | w writer |

Addams, Brian, 25 c
Addison, Nancy, 22 a
Ackerman, Bettye, 140 a
Aleata, Caroline, 108 c
Aleata, Edouard, 108 c
Aleata, Meg, 108 c
Alden, Kay, 31 p,w
Aldrich, Billy, 78 c
Aldrich, Carolee, 78 c
Aldrich, Erich, 78 c
Aldrich, Stephanie, 78 c
Aldrich, Steve, 78 c
Alexander, Denise, 87 a
Alexander, Millette, 107 a
Allan, Jed, 66 a
Allinson, Michael, 113 a
All My Children, 41
Ames, Rachel, 85 a
Anderson, Bob, 61 c
Anderson, Julie Banning, 61 c
Anderson, Phyllis, 63 c
Anderson, Richard Dean, 86 a
Andrews, Dana, 139 a
Aniston, John, 114 a
Another World, 12, 69
Arley, Jean, 108 p
Arnett, Terri, 84 c
Assante, Armand, 81 a
Astin, Patty Duke, 137 a
As the World Turns, 95

Backus, Richard, 16 a
Bailey, David, 75 a
Bain, Conrad, 139 a
Baldwin, Tom, 82 c
Baldwin, Tommy, 82 c
Banning, Natalie, 97 c
Banning, Scott, 61 c
Barcroft, Judith, 49 a

Barker, Margaret, 14 a
Barron, Jo, 115 c
Barron, Keith, 115 c
Barron, Patti, 115 c
Barrow, Bernard, 21 a
Battista, Lloyd, 113 a
Bauer, Bertha, 102 c
Bauer, Charita, 105 a
Bauer, Christina, 104 c
Bauer, Ed, 102 c
Bauer, Freddie, 103 c
Bauer, Hope, 102 c
Bauer, Jaime Lyn, 38 a
Bauer, Mike, 102 c
Baxter, Tom, 71 c
Beatty, Warren, 136 a
Beaulac, Dr. Seneca, 19 c
Beck, Donna, 43 c
Bedelia, Bonnie, 136 a
Belack, Doris, 56 a
Bell, Bill, 31 p,w
Bellini, Dr. Nick, 78 c
Benedict, Nick, 46 a
Bennett, Meg, 120 a
Benson, Robby, 142 a
Beradino, John, 85 a
Bergman, Janet, 116 c
Bergman, Marge, 116 c
Bergman, Stu, 116 c
Bergman, Stuart, Jr., 116 c
Berjer, Barbara, 106 a
Bethune, Zina, 142 a
Betz, Carl, 137 a
Breech, Kathryn, 57 a
Brent, Philip, 41 c
Brent, Ruth, 41 c
Brent, Ted, 41 c
Brewer, Jessie, 83 c
Brewer, Phil, 82 c
Brewster, Laurie, 13 c
Brooks, Chris, 31 c
Brooks, Leslie, 32 c

Brooks, Laurie, 32 c
Brooks, Peggy, 34 c
Brooks, Stuart, 31 c
Brown, Peter, 66 a
Browning, Susan, 30 a
Bruce, Lydia, 80 a
Bruder, Pat, 100 a
Bruns, Philip, 28 a

Campanella, Joseph, 143 a
Cannon, Dyan, 139 a
Carey, Macdonald, 63, 144, 145 a
Carr, Paul, 80 a
Carrington, Dennis, 73 c
Carrington, Eliot, 73 c
Carrington, Iris, 72 c
Carroll, Cindy, 143 a
Carson, Bruce, 117 c
Chapman, Judith, 101 a
Charney, Jordan, 59 a
Chancellor, Kay, 33 c
Chancellor, Phillip, 33 c
Chastain, Don, 85 a
Cheatham, Marie, 122 a
Clark, Cindy, 72 c
Clark, Ted, 70 c
Clarke, John, 64 a
Clayburgh, Jill, 140 a
Coco, Jimmy, 136 a
Colbert, Robert, 39 a
Coleman, Dabney, 29 a
Colenback, John, 99 a
Coleridge, Dr. Faith, 19 c
Coleridge, Jill, 18 c
Coleridge, Dr. Roger, 19 c
Collins, Wade, 117 c
Colman, Grant, 96 c
Colman, Joyce, 96 c
Colson, C. David, 101 a
Conley, Corine, 68 a

Convy, Bert, 143 a
Conway, Valerie, 96 c
Cook, Linda, 93 a
Cooney, Dennis, 101 a
Cooper, Jeanne, 37 a
Corby, Matt, 108 c
Corday, Ted, 95 a
Cory, Mackenzie, 70 c
Court, Geraldine, 81 a
Courtney, Jacqueline, 56 a
Craig, Anna, 51 c
Craig, Cathy, 51 c
Craig, Don, 62 c
Craig, Dr. Jim, 51 c
Craig, Megan, 51 c
Craig, Tony, 94 c
Cramer, Dr. Dorian, 53 c
Crawford, Betsy, 109 c
Crawford, Dr. Tom, 109 c
Crompton, Forrest, 92 a
Cunningham, John, 120 a
Curtis, George, 32 c
Curtis, Jack, 35 c
Curtis, Joann, 35 c
Curtis, Dr. Neil, 62 c
Cushing, Austin, 13 c
Cushing, Edith, 12 c
Cushing, Megan, 13 c
Cushing, Richard, 12 c

Dallas, Johnny, 90 c
Dallas, Johnny, Jr., 90 c
Dancy, Joan, 76 c
Dante, Dr. Mark, 84 c
Dante, Mary Ellen, 84 c
Davis, Dr. Althea, 77 c
Davis, Kitty Shea, 46 c
Davis, Nick, 42 c
Davis, Penny, 78 c
Davis, Rachel, 70 c
Dawson, Vicky, 16 a

149

Days of Our Lives, 60
DeHaven, Gloria, 29 a
Delaney, Robert, 73 c
Dennis, Sandy, 139 a
Dickson, Brenda, 37 a
Dixon, John, 96 c
Dixon, Kim, 96 c
Doctors, The, 76
Donahue, Elinor, 143 a
Donahue, Troy, 137 a
Douglas, James, 99 a
Dow, Tony, 143 a
Downs, Ernie, 72 c
Drake, Adam, 90 c
Driver, John, 91 a
DuBois, Ja'net, 143 a
Duffy, Julia, 81 a
Dufour, Val, 122 a
Duncan, Sandy, 137 a
Durning, Charles, 140 a

Edge of Night, The, 89
Eliot, Brad, 32 c
Englund, Patricia, 14 a
Estrin, Patricia, 14 a
Evans, Damon, 143 a
Evans, Dr. Marlena, 61 c

Fairchild, Morgan, 122 a
Falk, Peter, 136 a
Farraday, Timmy, 90 c
Faulkner, Cameron, 84 c
Faulkner, Leslie, 84 c
Fenelli, Jack, 20 c
Ferguson, Connie, 13 c
Fernwood Flasher, 24 c
Fickett, Mary, 46, 144 a
First 100 Years, The, 4
Fitzgerald, Geraldine, 139 a
Flannery, Susan, 140, 145 a
Flemming, Felicia, 100 c
Fletcher, Billy, 105 c
Fletcher, Peggy, 104 c
Flood, Ann, 92 a
Ford, Constance, 75 a
Forsyth, Rosemary, 64 a
Forsythe, Henderson, 100 a
Foster, Bill, 36 c
Foster, Greg, 31 c
Foster, Liz, 36 c
Foster, Snapper, 31 c
Frame, Jamie, 70 c
Frame, Steven, 70 c
Frame, Willis, 71 c
Franklin, Hugh, 49 a
Frann, Mary, 66 a
Fulton, Eileen, 99, 134 a

Gabriel, John, 22, 135 a
Gallagher, Helen, 21, 145 a

Gallison, Joe, 66 a
General Hospital, 82
Gifford, Amy, 13 c
Gimble, Garth, 26 c
Gimble, Pat, 26 c
Glass, Katherine, 57 a
Goodman, Dody, 27 a
Gordon, Gerald, 88 a
Gorney, Karen, 48 a
Granger, Farley, 59 a
Grant, Heather, 84 c
Grant, Lee, 136 a
Green, Dorothy, 39 a
Gregory, Michael, 86 a
Gregory, Roxanne, 112 a
Groh, David, 139 a
Groome, Malcolm, 21 a
Guiding Light, 5, 102

Haggers, Charlie, 25 c
Haggers, Loretta, 25 c
Hagman, Larry, 139 a
Haines, Larry, 119, 145 a
Hall, Deidre, 66 a
Hallick, Tom, 36 a
Halsey, Brett, 87 a
Hamilton, Desmond, 13 c
Hamilton, Margaret, 142 a
Hanson, Maggie, 61 c
Hanson, Marty, 61 c
Harben, Chandler Hill, 112 a
Hardy, Audrey, 82 c
Hardy, Dr. Steve, 82 c
Harmon, Jennifer, 56 a
Harney, Susan, 73 a
Harper, Ben, 109 c
Harper, Dianne, 14 a
Harper, Ellie, 116 c
Hart, Meg, 108 c
Hartman, Heather, 24 c
Hartman, Mary, 23 c
Hartman, Tom, 23 c
Hasselhoff, David, 36 a
Hastings, Don, 98 a
Hatch, Richard, 140 a
Hayes, Bill, 65, 134 a
Hayes, Susan Seaforth, 65 a
Hays, Kathryn, 99 a
Heberle, Kay, 39 a
Heffernan, John, 14 a
Heineman, Laurie, 75 a
Henderson, Brandy, 91 c
Henderson, Mark, 33 a
Herrera, Anthony, 39 a
Higgins, Joel, 120 a
Hobart, Dr. Jim, 82 c
Hoffman, Dustin, 136 a
Horton, Maggie, 61 c
Horton, Alice, 60 c
Horton, Bill, 60 c
Horton, Jennifer Rose, 61 c
Horton, Laura, 60 c

Horton, Marie, 60 c
Horton, Mickey, 60 c
Horton, Mike, 60 c
Horton, Dr. Tom, 60 c
Horton, Tom, Jr., 60 c
Howard, Amanda, 62 c
Hubbard, Elizabeth, 81, 144 a
Huebing, Craig, 86, 133 a
Hughes, Barnard, 143 a
Hughes, Bob, 95 c
Hughes, Chris, 95 c
Hughes, Don, 95 c
Hughes, Jennifer, 95 c
Hughes, Lisa Miller, 95 c
Hughes, Nancy, 95 c
Hughes, Penny, 95 c
Hughes, Tom, 95 c
Hulswit, Mart, 105 a

Jackson, Kate, 139 a
Jackson, Leslie, 102 c
Jackson, Dr. Steve, 102 c
James, Francesca, 50 a
Jamison, Kevin, 89 c
Jarvis, Graham, 29 a
Jeeter, Rev. Jimmy Joe, 26 c
Jeeter, Merle, 26 c
Jeffers, Ann, 104 c
Jenkins, Florence Andrews, 82 c
Johnson, Detective, 25 c
Jones, Christine, 16 a
Jones, James Earl, 142 a
Jordan, Bobbie, 88 a
Jordan, Dr. Craig, 89 c
Joyce, Stephen, 15 a

Kane, Mona, 43 c
Karr, Laurie, 90 c
Karr, Mike, 90 c
Karr, Nancy, 90 c
Karras, Dr. Christina, 45 c
Kaslo, Amy, 117 c
Kaslo, Steve, 117 c
Kayzer, Beau, 37, 133 a
Keane, Teri, 59 a
Keith, Larry, 49 a
Kemp, Elizabeth, 112 a
Kendall, Brian, 52 c
Kendall, Patricia, 52 c
Kerwin, Brian, 40 a
Kibbee, Lois, 92 a
Kilian, Victor, 28 a
Kimball, George, 13 c
Knotts, Don, 136 a
Kramer, Mandel, 91 a
Kristin, Ilene, 21 a

Labine, Claire, 6 a
Lacy, Jerry, 112 a

Ladd, Diane, 137 a
LaGioia, John, 93 a
Lamont, Diana, 110 c
Lamont, Charles, 110 c
Lamonte, Vic, 90 c
La Piere, Georgann, 86 a
Larimer, Dr. Ann, 78 c
Larkin, Grandpa, 24 c
Lasser, Louise, 23, 27 a
Latimer, Rick, 109 c
Lear, Norman, 23 p
Lemay, Harding, 12 p
Levin, Michael, 22 a
Lincoln, Pamela, 114 a
Linden, Hal, 139 a
Lindley, Audra, 140 a
Lord, Tony, 51 c
Lord, Victor, 51 c
Love of Life, 3, 6, 108
Lovers and Friends, 12
Lovett, Arlene, 109 c
Lovett, Carrie, 110 c
Lucci, Susan, 49 a
Lynde, Janice, 134 a

MacDonnell, Ray, 46 a
MacLaughlin, Don, 98 a
MacRae, Ellen, 137 a
Mallory, Edward, 64 a
Manners, Barbara, 12 c
Marceau, Bill, 89 c
Marceau, Martha, 89 c
Marceau, Phoebe, 89 c
Marchand, Nancy, 14 a
Marcovicci, Andrea, 139 a
Marlowe, Hugh, 73 a
Martin, Elizabeth, 45 c
Martin, Erica Kane, 42 c
Martin, Dr. Joseph, 41 c
Martin, Jeff, 41 c
Martin, Paul, 44 c
Martin, Ruth, 41 c
Martin, Tara, 41 c
Mary Hartman, Mary Hartman, 23
Mason, Margaret, 65 a
Mason, Marsha, 140 a
Masters, Marie, 99 a
Matthews, Alice, 69 c
Matthews, Jim, 69 c
Matthews, Mary, 69 c
Matthews, Pat, 69 c
Matthews, Russ, 69 c
May, Donald, 93 a
Mayer, Paul Avila, 6 w
McCarthy, Julianna, 40 a
McClanahan, Rue, 139 a
McConnell, Judith, 99 a
McCook, John, 38, 133 a
McCormack, Patty, 139 a
McGowan, Ada Davis, 72 c
McGowan, Gil, 72 c

McGowan, Nancy, 72 c
McGuire, Maeve, 94 a
McGuire, Sally, 31 c
McKechnie, Donna, 137 a
McKinsey, Beverlee, 75 a
McLaughlin, Emily, 86 a
Mercer, Marion, 30 a
Merriwether, Lee, 142 a
Milli, Robert, 106 a
Mills, Donna, 139 a
Moore, Jonathan, 114 a
Muldaur, Diana, 139 a
Mulgrew, Kate, 22 a
Mull, Martin, 30 a
Mullavey, Greg, 27 a
Murray, Peg, 113 a
Myers, Fran, 106 a

Newman, Barry, 140 a
Norris, Andrew, 104 c
Norris, Barbara, 104 c
Norris, Holly, 103 c
Norris, Kenneth, 104 c
Norris, Stanley, 103 c
Nouri, Michael, 120, 134 a

O'Brien, David, 81 a
O'Connor, Glynnis, 142 a
O'Neil, Patrick, 142 a
One Life to Live, 51

Pace, Jennifer, 117 c
Pace, Stephanie, 118 c
Parker, Jameson, 57 a
Patterson, Lee, 57 a
Patterson, Linda, 61 c
Penbarthy, Beverly, 74 a
Peters, Audrey, 111 a
Peters, Dr. Greg, 62 c
Phillips, Eric, 116 c
Phillips, Irna, 95 w
Phillips, Jennifer Pace, 118 c
Phillips, Kathy, 116 c
Phillips, Laurie, 116 c
Phillips, Scott, 116 c
Pinkerton, Nancy, 57 a
Place, Mary Kay, 29, 135 a
Plumb, Flora, 15 a
Polen, Nat, 55 a
Powers, Dr. Maggie, 76 c
Powers, Dr. Matt, 76 c
Powers, Michael Paul, 77 c
Powers, Mike, 77 c
Powers, Toni, 77 c
Prentiss, Lance, 33 c
Prentiss, Vanessa, 34 c
Preston, J.A., 139 a
Pritchett, James, 80 a

Rahn, Patsy, 87 a
Ramsey, David, 15 a
Randall, Tony, 137 a
Randell, Ron, 14 a
Randolph, John, 71 c
Randolph, Marianna, 71 c
Randolph, Michael, 71 c
Rauch, Paul, 12 w
Raven, Paul, 108 c
Ray, Leslie, 81 a
Reid, Frances, 64 a
Reid, Woody, 117 c
Reinholt, George, 56 a
Rettig, Tommy, 143 a
Reynolds, Andrea, 115 c
Reynolds, Brock, 33 c
Reynolds, Sam, 115 c
Riley, Joe, 51 c
Riley, Kevin, 53 c
Riley, Victoria Lord, 52 c
Rittenhouse, Wanda, 26 c
Roberts, Tony, 139 a
Robinson, Andrew, 21 a
Rodell, Barbara, 98 a
Rogers, Suzanne, 65 a
Rogers, Wayne, 140 a
Rolle, Esther, 139 a
Rose, Jane, 139 a
Ross, Marion, 137 a
Rowland, Jada, 81 a
Russell, Ian, 110 c
Russom, Leon, 74 a
Ruthledge, Rev. Mr., 102 c
Ryan, Delia, 18 c
Ryan, Frank, 8, 18 c
Ryan, Johnny, 7, 17 c
Ryan, Johnny, II, 18 c
Ryan, Kathleen, 18 c
Ryan, Maeve, 17 c
Ryan, Mary, 18 c
Ryan, Michael, 74 a
Ryan, Patrick, 18 c
Ryan, Siobhan, 18 c
Ryan's Hope, 6, 17

Saint, Eva Marie, 137 a
Saxton, Bentley, 13 c
Saxton, Eleanor, 13 c
Saxton, Jason, 13 c
Saxton, Josie, 13 c
Saxton, Lester, 13 c
Saxton, Rhett, 13 c
Saxton, Tessa, 13 c
Scheider, Roy, 139 a
Schnabel, Stefan, 105 a
Scott, Debralee, 28 a
Scott, Draper, 91 c
Search for Tomorrow, 3, 4, 115
Sherman, Courtney, 119 a
Shumway, George, 25 c
Shumway, Kathy, 25 c

Schumway, Martha, 24 c
Siegel, Jenny, 54 c
Siegel, Tim, 54 c
Simon, Peter, 119 a
Slater, Ray, 110 c
Slezak, Erika, 57 a
Slocum, Sophia, 13 c
Sloan, David, 118 c
Solow, Pamela, 39 a
Sondergaard, Gale, 139 a
Stallings, Carol Hughes, 97 c
Stallings, Jay, 97 c
Starrett, Valerie, 86 a
Sterling, Bruce, 108 c
Sterling, Vanessa, 108 c
Stevens, K.T., 38 a
Stewart, Dan, 96 c
Stewart, David, 97 c
Stewart, Don, 105, 133 a
Stewart, Ellen, 97 c
Stewart, Susan, 96 c
Stewart, Trish, 36 a
Storm, Michael, 57 a
Strasser, Robin, 49 a
Streeter, Dr. Adam, 84 c
Stuart, Mary, 118, 132, 144 a
Sullivan, Susan, 143 a
Summers, Dr. Paul, 76 c
Sweet, Dolph, 75 a

Taggart, Millee, 120 a
Talbot, Nita, 136 a
Tate, Arthur, 115 c
Taylor, Diana, 82 c
Taylor, Dr. Peter, 83 c
Thomas, Richard, 139 a
Thorpe, Adam, 104 c
Thorpe, Roger, 103 c
Thorton, Dr. David, 45 c
Tolksdorf, Birgitta, 113 a
Tomme, Ron, 112 a
Travis, Nicole, 91 c
Twelvetrees, Billy, 24 c
Tyler, Anne, 43 c
Tyler, Dr. Charles, 43 c
Tyler, Chuck, 42 c
Tyler, Lincoln, 43 c
Tyler, Phoebe, 43 c
Tyson, Cecily, 142 a

Van Devere, Trish, 139 a
Van Patten, Dick 142 a
Van Vleet, Richard, 48 a
Vernon, Brad, 54 c
Vernon, Naomi, 54 c
Vernon, Dr. Will, 54 c
de Villiers, Thomas, 108 p
Vincente, Marcy, 116 c
Vincente, Dr. Tony, 115 c

Wagner, Helen, 98 a
Walter, Jessica, 136 a
Walter, Rita McLaughlin, 101 a
Walton, Danny, 117 c
Walton, Gary, 117 c
Walton, Janet Bergman, 117 c
Walton, Liza, 117 c
Waring, Charlotte, 103 c
Warren, Linda, 139 a
Warrick, Lee, 88 a
Warrick, Ruth, 49, 133 c
Washam, Wisner, 49 w
Watson, Douglass, 74 a
Watt, Billie Lou, 119 a
Watts, Sharlene, 72 c
Weaver, Patty, 135 a
Webber, Dr. Jeff, 83 c
Webber, Dr. Monica, 83 c
Webber, Rick, 83 c
Weber, Rick, 112 a
Wells, Stacy, 76 c
Werner, Dr. Joe, 105 c
Werner, Dr. Karen, 78 c
Werner, Dr. Sara, 105 c
Werner, T.J., 105 c
West, Martin, 98 a
Where the Heart Is, 6
White, Peter, 50 a
Whitney, Geraldine, 89 c
Wiggins, Tudi, 112 a
Williams, Addie, 61 c
Williams, Billy Dee, 142 a
Williams, Doug, 61 c
Williams, Hope, 62 c
Williams, Kim, 62 c
Wilson, Sandy, 95 c
Winsor, Roy, 3 p
Wolek, Danny, 53 c
Wolek, Karen, 54 c
Wolek, Larry, 53 c
Wolek, Meredith, 53 c
Wolek, Vincent, 53 c
Wolek, Wanda, 55 c
Wyatt, Eunice, 118 c
Wyatt, John, 118 c
Wyatt, Annie, 24 c
Wyndham, Anne, 120 a
Wyndham, Victoria, 73 a

de Young, Cliff, 137 a
Young and the Restless, The, 31

Zaslow, Michael, 106 a
Zimbalist, Efrem, Jr., 139 a

Index 151